Mr & Mrs Purcell
4/07

D0118401

EXALTING HIS WORD

*LET THE BIBLE
IN YOUR HANDS
BE HIS POWER
IN YOUR LIFE!*

SHELLEY QUINN

Pacific Press® Publishing Association
Nampa, Idaho
Oshawa, Ontario, Canada
www.pacificpress.com

3ABN BOOKS

P. O. Box 220
West Frankfort, Illinois
www.3ABN.org

Designed by Steve Nelson
Cover photo by Steve Nelson

Copyright © 2006 by
Shelley J. Quinn

Printed in the United States of America
All rights reserved

Scripture quotations used in this book are marked as follows:

NKJV—The New King James Version, copyright © 1979, 1980, 1982 by Thomas Nelson, Inc.,
Publishers. Used by permission.

AMP—THE AMPLIFIED BIBLE, Old Testament copyright © 1965, 1987 by
the Zondervan Corporation. The Amplified New Testament copyright © 1958, 1987 by The
Lockman Foundation. Used by permission.

NIV—The Holy Bible, New International Version, copyright © 1973, 1978, 1984, International
Bible Society. Used by permission of Zondervan Bible Publishers.

All unmarked Scripture quotations are taken from The Authorized King James Version
of the Bible.

In all cases the emphasis within Scripture quotations has been supplied by the author.

Additional copies of this book are available from two locations:
3ABN: Call 1-800-752-3226 or visit www.3abn.org
Adventist Book Centers: Call 1-800-765-6855
or visit www.adventistbookcenter.com

3ABN Books is dedicated to bringing you the best in published materials consistent with the
mission of Three Angels Broadcasting Network. Our goal is to uplift Jesus through books,
audio, and video materials by our family of 3ABN presenters. Our in-depth Bible study guides,
devotionals, biographies, and lifestyle materials promote the whole person in health and the
mending of broken people. For more information, call 616-627-4651 or visit 3ABN's Web site:
www.3ABN.org

ISBN: 0-8163-2147-7
ISBN 13: 9780816321476

06 07 08 09 10 • 5 4 3 2 1

Dedication

To all who long
to know God's plan of love.

To all who want
a more intimate relationship
with God.

To all who look
for an abundant life and
power to walk in Christ's footsteps.

Acknowledgments

Glory to God for drawing me out of darkness and into the marvelous light of His Word. Glory to Him for revealing that which was previously fenced in and hidden from me. All praise to Jesus Christ, who paid my penalty at the cruel cross of Calvary. All praise to Him who causes me to be all that He has called me to be.

To my husband, JD—thank you for loving me as Christ loves the church. You make it easy for me to submit to your leadership, because you always have my best interests in mind and encourage my growth. In becoming your wife, I was blessed; in sharing your life, I am privileged. I'm so glad we have eternity to spend together.

To Danny Shelton—thank you for recognizing God's call on my life and for giving me the opportunity to produce the *Exalting His Word* series on Three Angels Broadcasting Network. You made it possible to share this God-given teaching with the world, and I am most grateful. Your personal faith-walk with God is a constant source of encouragement to me.

To my sister in Christ, Pat Mudgett—thank you for giving your time so freely to proofread this book. Most of all, thanks for your enthusiastic encouragement—a true blessing from God.

Contents

Preparing Good Soil for Planting
Broadcasting the Seed of His Word
Receiving and Retaining His Promises
Persevering to Produce a Harvest
Harvest Hope

A Profound, Yet Simple Teaching
English Translations
Rhema Affirmations Defined
Creative Word Power

Rhema Confession Increases Our Faith
The *Rhema* Word Is Our Spiritual Nutrition
The *Rhema* Word Sustains and Upholds Us
Rhema Washes Away the Influences of the World
The *Rhema* Word Is the Sword of the Spirit
Rhema Increases the Effectiveness of Prayer
No *Rhema* Word Is Impossible of Fulfillment
It's Dangerous to Reject the *Rhema* Word
The Power of "I Am"
Distilled Wisdom

The Sweet Healing Waters
A Cup of Water
Sanctified Minds
What Are We Exalting?
Increase the Measure of Your Expectancy
His Word Is Final

About the Author

Shelley Quinn is speaker and co-director for Word Warrior Ministries. As a Christian author and Bible teacher, she travels the United States and abroad preaching the gospel of Christ at revivals, retreats, and camp meetings. Her teaching revolves around knowing who we are "in Christ," expanding our vision of who God is, and understanding how to develop an intimate personal relationship with the Lord.

Shelley is the New Program Development Manager at Three Angels Broadcasting Network (3ABN). She also hosts *Exalting His Word* and other programs seen around the world on 3ABN. With Danny Shelton, the network's president, Shelley co-authored the best-selling books *The Antichrist Agenda* and *Ten Commandments Twice Removed.*

Shelley and her husband, JD, work side-by-side in full-time ministry.

Section One

A Personal Victory

Chapter One
A New Beginning

I'll never forget an overnight stay with a dear friend. For years, phone wires had been our only thread of connection. We were eager to meet face to face again (if for nothing else than to see how the ravages of time had taken their toll on us). My hectic travel schedule had foiled our frequently proposed reunion plans, but now I was in her area on ministry business, and we were finally together again.

The comfort of our close relationship rapidly erased the time we had been apart. We chatted and chirped for hours. After catching up on recent events, the conversation took a turn I had hoped to avoid. "Remember when . . . ?" As soon as those words escaped her mouth, I knew I was in trouble. Remembering our past escapades, her face lighted with enthusiasm. Mine flushed hot with shame.

Our friendship had sprouted in our late twenties, during an interval when I had left the church. I was knee-deep in the ways of the world, and my behavior then fell far short of God's approval. Now I interrupted her, saying, "Those were my B.C. (Before Christ) days; let's not talk about them."

Shocked, she insisted I had always been a Christian. After I tried to explain the difference between knowing *about* God and living *for* Him, she said, "Well, at least you have to agree those early years were fun." I couldn't agree. What she considered fond memories, I regarded as a time of reckless folly.

In the past, it seemed to me that God's "Highway of Holiness"[1] was poorly paved and marked. I stumbled into potholes. I took several wrong exits that ended in roadblocks. After each hair-raising episode, my loving Lord reached out and guided me back to His path of life. Hand in hand, I walked happily with my Savior for long stretches of the way. Then, incredibly, I would again withdraw my hand from His.

When I started wandering around under my own direction again, confusion soon clouded my mind. I couldn't see the narrow path that Christ asked me to follow. It baffled me when my passion for Christ as my "first love"[2] faded. Why did the joy drain from my times of Bible study? Why did prayer become stiff and mechanical? No one else in my church spoke of this awkward condition, so I mastered the cover-up of verbal camouflage—I gave God lip service without yielding daily control to Him.

I've finally learned the secret of keeping my hand in God's hand and walking so near to Him that I sense His heartbeat. I recognize that I'm absolutely dependent upon the transforming power of His Spirit and His Word working within me.

Finally, disregard for His direction caused me to follow a destructive path. I slammed into a barricade, and then, stunned and ashamed, I limped away—away from Christ. This is embarrassing to admit, but if I had been on trial, accused of being a believer in Christ during that time in my life, I doubt anyone could have produced sufficient evidence to convict me.

Even now, shame strikes at my heart if I visit the gallery of my past. But thankfully, the Lord has taught me to return my focus rapidly to Him. As my Savior's voice reassures me, "You are forgiven," He keeps me from falling into the pit of condemnation. A quick sidestep gets me past that snare of the devil.

God's grace equips me to press forward in assurance of His power to keep my feet from slipping off track again. And my grateful heart overflows with a constant offering of thanksgiving and praise to the God of new beginnings.

I've finally learned the secret of keeping my hand in God's hand and walking so near to Him that I sense His heartbeat. I recognize that I'm absolutely dependent upon the transforming power of His Spirit and His Word working within me. Without His Spirit, I cannot understand His Word. Without His Word operating in my heart, I can't follow in His footsteps.

God has revealed to me the central mystery of Christian life—the triumphant entry of His Word. The miracle-working power of God's Word is His way of transforming me into His image. Knowing this, I've learned to exalt His Word above all things. God's Word is my most special treasure in life.

It pays to know this: The secret of success for all humanity is **exalting His Word.**

Exalting His Word

In Psalm 138:2, the Bible says that God exalts His name and His word above all else. It continues to say that God magnifies His word even above His name. The bottom line is this—**God exalts His Word above everything.** That means nothing is more important to Him. As Commander-in-Chief, God has promoted His Word to the highest rank of importance. He empowers His Word with greater force than anything else. God has granted creative, life-giving power to His Word—power to accomplish all of His will.

Almighty God has assigned the highest position of praise to His Word. Just as our Creator glorifies His Word, so should we.

Why? The Bible explains it to us. Because "In the beginning was the Word, and the Word was with God, and the Word was God. . . . In Him was life; and the life was the light of men [humanity]. . . . The Word became flesh and dwelt among us",[3] and sacrificed His lifeblood for us. Jesus Christ was, is, and ever will be, the living Word of God. Even at Christ's return, at the Second Coming, the Bible declares He is the Word of God.

> He was clothed with a robe dipped in blood,
> and His name is called **the Word of God.** . . .
> And He has on His robe and on His thigh a name written:
> KING OF KINGS AND LORD OF LORDS
> *(Revelation 19:13, 16, NKJV).*

Christ is the Word of Life.[4] Everything He is, the Word of the Bible is also. He is love, light, life, truth, and power. The Bible is love, light, life, truth, and power.

How privileged we are to hold a Bible in our hands—we are grasping the hand of God, and He will lead us.

God exalts His Word to the greatest place of importance. Would you agree with me that His Word should be our top priority also?

I'm writing this book to help you grasp the true meaning of "exalting His Word." I hope to help you better understand why God has

"You have exalted above all else Your name and Your word, and You have magnified Your word above all Your name"

(Psalm 138:2, AMP).

elevated His Word to the place of highest rank and honor. Equally important, the purpose of this study is to reveal why and how you can please God by giving His Word the highest place in your life.

This is a life-changing study. We have this assurance based on the authority of God's Word. Do you want a closer walk with Jesus? Do you want the joy of your salvation restored to you? Are you ready to overcome a powerless spiritual

> *Either I walk in the power of God's Word and His Spirit, or I limp through the day staggering under the weight of my earthly burdens.*

condition? If you will take to heart the lessons in this book, God will do a great work in you.

I first began sharing these concepts in 1996 and marveled at the power of God's Word to transform lives as I witnessed hundreds of Christians develop a closer walk with God. Since *Exalting His Word* began airing on the Three Angels Broadcasting Network (3ABN) in 2002, thousands of Christians have eagerly embraced this teaching. Their testimonies confirm the power of exalting His Word. I also testify to this truth by my own changed life. God gave me a new beginning by leading me through this study and opening my understanding.

Pressing forward

Reflecting on my Christian walk, I recognize that I daily live in one of two conditions. I'm either powerful or pitiful. Either I walk in the power of God's Word and His Spirit, or I limp through the day staggering under the weight of my earthly burdens.

Life is a messy affair. If I try to live for Christ in my limited human strength and understanding, I'm to be pitied. I've forgotten my Lord's advice: "Without Me you can do nothing."[5] The pitiful condition of my earlier Christian experience was the result of self-propelled performance. Not knowing how to achieve and sustain maturity in Christ, I found myself in the old routine of "three steps forward—two steps back."

I felt like a child trying to walk up the "down" escalator. Have you ever seen one at play like this? With great enthusiasm, he meets the challenge of the mechanical stairs flowing downward. Usually, he scrambles halfway up the moving staircase. Then, resting for a moment, he is carried back in the opposite direction. As he nears the bottom, the upward scramble begins again.

Watching children do this, I've noted something interesting. Rarely do they press forward all the way to the top and step off the escalator. Most often, they perform the upward effort, stop their advancement, and ride the downward flow. Then they struggle up a similar distance and backslide again. When they finally weary of the game, they stop.

Can you see a comparison between our Christian walk and this escalator scene? Christians struggle against the downward trend of the world system. It's just like trying to walk up a "down" escalator. If we stop advancing, we start backsliding. If we're startled into awareness of lost ground, we start pressing forward—unless we've grown exhausted by the effort.

Oh, how we must guard our hearts so that we don't weary of the upward race! Unchecked backsliding can cost us our relationship with Christ. It doesn't have to be this way. He will give us the victory, if we will just let Him. We must press forward in determination to make it to the top in Christlike maturity—depending on His power to overcome all of our obstacles.

Jesus said, "My grace is sufficient for you, for My power is made perfect in your weakness."[6] He never intended for us to rely on limited human strength. We can't press forward without His power. Backsliding can't be prevented without His power. "Apart from me, you can do nothing."[7] Remember the Savior's words? Only the power of Christ overcomes our weakness. Only by His power are we able to do what He asks us to do. Our hope is found in absolute dependence upon God.

God is the God of new beginnings

It's true, God is the God of new beginnings. His love and compassion never fail, and His mercies are new every morning.[8]

Have you grown weary and realized you're backsliding? He will renew your strength, exchanging His strength for yours.[9] Have you made a wrong turn and find yourself on a crooked road? Cry out for direction. He will guide you back to His path of life.[10] Is there an obstacle preventing you from drawing near to the Lord? He desires to remove it—and He will, if you give Him permission.

Our hope is found in absolute dependence upon God.

God has a plan for our lives, and it's better than the one we've been living.[11] In reality, His plan is dramatically different from the one most of us follow. In His unconditional love and infinite wisdom, He designed a plan so simple that anyone can share in it.

The Word of God reveals the plan and actually brings to life God's purposes for us. Jesus Christ is the mediator of this plan.[12] He brings us into agreement with God and reconciles our differences.[13]

To understand reconciliation in its simplest terms, let's compare it to our bank account. Because of sin, our account with God has been overdrawn. There is no way we can pay the debt. Christ paid our debt at the cross of Calvary—He deposited His righteousness into our account to cover our deficit. Then God sent the Holy Spirit to be our helper. By the Spirit's power operating within us, God can work out His plan for our lives.

In Christ, God will do for us what we cannot do for ourselves. God wants to work out His will in us. He wants to transform us by the infused power of His Word and His Spirit. He plans to *cause* us to be all He has *called* us to be.[14]

Our part in this plan is to receive His power and surrender to His leading. The Bible tells us the true children of God are those led by His Spirit.[15] But how do we follow His leading? What God asks of you and me is that we be teachable, cooperating and relying completely on Him.

"So then . . . make every effort to be found spotless, blameless and at peace with him."[16] Participation in God's plan does require us to exert energy. Still it's an effort empowered by the Word and the Holy Spirit. God knows that we can't perfect our walk with Him by human effort.[17] It has to be a "faith walk" and not a "flesh walk."

> *In Christ, God will do for us what we cannot do for ourselves.*

Daily we choose whom we will serve—self or God.[18] I have discovered that even when we dedicate our lives to God, we may still suffer days dedicated to self-interest. How much more joyful we would be if we surrendered each day to His marvelous love and plan for our lives!

Each day is a new beginning with God. We cannot base our future on previous failures or successes.

> When the righteous turns from his righteousness and commits iniquity,
> he shall die because of it.
> But when the wicked turns from his wickedness and does what is lawful
> and right, he shall live because of it
> *(Ezekiel 33:18, 19, NKJV).*

Forget the former things;
do not dwell on the past.
See, I am doing a new thing!
Now it springs up; do you not perceive it?
I am making a way in the desert
and streams in the wasteland
(Isaiah 43:18, 19, NIV).

God wants to give you the gift of a new beginning.
Will you receive it?

References

1. Isaiah 35:8, NKJV.
2. Revelation 2:4, NKJV.
3. John 1:1, 4, 14, NKJV.
4. 1 John 1:1.
5. John 15:5, NKJV.
6. 2 Corinthians 12:9, NIV.
7. John 15:5, NIV.
8. Lamentations 3:22, 23.
9. Isaiah 40:31.
10. Psalm 16:11.
11. Jeremiah 29:11.
12. 1 Timothy 2:5.
13. 2 Corinthians 5:19.
14. Philippians 2:13.
15. Romans 8:14.
16. 2 Peter 3:14, NIV.
17. Galatians 3:3.
18. Joshua 24:15.

Chapter Two
God's Word Is Life to Me

I became involved in part-time ministry in 1987. Any time the doors of my non-denominational church opened, I was there—eager to participate. Many teachings were stored in my mind. I thought I understood God's plan. Yet, it wasn't until eight years later this truth was unveiled: God's Word is *life* to me.

"My Words are not idle words. My Word is life unto you."[1]

In 1995, what God declared to me forever changed my viewpoint. His words came when I was gripped in the vise of a Job experience. Like Job, the ancient patriarch of the Bible, life as I had known it had vanished. My health, home, family members, and friends had all fallen along the wayside. My trial wasn't as dramatic as poor Job's—but it was too close for comfort. Over the span of one year, I was tested in the furnace of affliction.

The comforts and contentment of life had been washing away, piece by battered piece. I was suffering from vertigo, a tormenting condition of dizziness that makes you feel like your environment is whirling. My case was relentless. My surroundings seemed to spin at 120 revolutions a minute, twenty-four hours a day—whether I stood, sat, or lay down.

Walking became an exhausting struggle. Nausea convulsed my stomach constantly. I couldn't read or watch television because my pupils were constricted, and my vision was blurred. Soon, I stammered when I tried to talk. I wondered, *Have I suffered a stroke?*

My condition confounded the wisdom of medical science and left my doctors clueless. Nothing they prescribed brought relief. The only effect of multiple steroid treatments was a thirty-five pound weight gain, which added to the clumsiness I already felt. I became self-conscious when I tried to walk or talk. Embarrassed to be seen in public, I began to withdraw—wanting to crawl off to a solitary place, like a wounded dog making an exit with his tail tucked between his legs.

Solitude was what I wanted, and solitude was what I got. When my husband, JD, started a new business that required extensive travel, I was relieved to spend several months coping with my condition alone. At least this way JD didn't have to witness my struggle, and that made me feel like less of a burden.

Three months into my illness, I found myself having to pack and store our belongings. We had decided to move from Houston to JD's hometown. But the relocation didn't go at all as planned. An interim stay with loving in-laws became a semi-permanent and awkward arrangement.

JD and I were apart for weeks at a time. I felt an intense loneliness, amplified by the absence of my Houston church family and friends. More than that, I was feeling trapped by circumstances. The swirling hurricane called vertigo had then held me prisoner for eight months, without a moment of reprieve. None of my family realized the extremes of my physical and emotional challenges. I masked the truth with a smile.

> *None of my family realized the extremes of my physical and emotional challenges. I masked the truth with a smile.*

As I lay in bed one night, an unexpected and ominous thought began to thunder in my mind. *Now I understand why you tried it, Mama.* My mother had attempted suicide several times when I was a child. For years I had tried to comprehend why anyone would dare such a desperate act, but no life experience had helped me gain insight—until now. In bleak darkness, I saw more clearly than ever before. Suicide was a simple answer to a complex question. Mama had lost all hope. Without hope, life doesn't seem worth the struggle.

A gripping panic narrowed my focus. Though I wasn't considering the act of suicide, I was experiencing an emotional identification that grasped the "why" of it. *If I can sink this low, what if I sink lower? Oh, help me, Lord!* I wanted to pray more, but words wouldn't come. Frightening thoughts hazed my senses as the night wore on.

The next morning I staggered through my daily routine in deep thought. I had always been so stable-minded. How had I reached this unfamiliar place in my reasoning? Fear seized my heart. *Am I capable of following in my mother's footsteps? Is my situation really hopeless?* It was time for a serious talk with the Lord.

Lord, I'd rather be in extreme pain than to suffer this debilitating vertigo. It was a thought, more than a prayer. Prayer time had become another casualty of this battle, gradually reduced to moments of brooding. Always before, prayer was a trusted lifeline . . . but now? *I'm drowning emotionally, and I don't know how to reach out to the Lord.*

Drawing a deep breath, I uttered, "Help, Lord!" Again I made the agonizing effort, "Please, Father, help me." Nothing more would come.

Suddenly I heard a still, small voice.[2] It wasn't audible—it was more like thoughts being impressed upon my mind. Yet it was a voice, and I knew Who it was. God said, "I . . . set before you life and death . . . choose life."[3] *I have chosen life, Father. Jesus Christ is my Savior. If you mean anything more than that, You will have to explain it to me. I'm in no condition to figure it out.*

> You must persevere, so that after you've done the will of God, you'll receive what He has promised
> (Hebrews 10:36, paraphrased).

He spoke again. "My Words are not idle words. My Word is life unto you. Anything that does not line up in agreement with My Word is nothing more than a pretentious lie of the enemy.[4] If you choose to believe My Word, you choose life. If you doubt My Word—if you believe the deception of the evil one— you have chosen death."

The Lord directed me to go to the Bible, seek out His promises related to healing and new beginnings, and hold fast to these. He instructed me to claim His promises, speaking His Word aloud daily. Faith comes by hearing.[5]

Miracles follow faith

With great hope, I opened my Bible for the first time in many months. Straining to focus, I jotted down verse references. I spoke each Scripture aloud, finishing with Hebrews 10:36, "You must persevere, so that after you've done the will of God, you'll receive what He has promised."

Night after night, I rehearsed the Scriptures. Soon I was inspired to "write the vision and make it plain."[6] In handwriting now barely legible, I scribbled Scripture promises on a yellow legal pad, adding to the list nightly. As I recited these with reverent devotion, I struggled with self-doubt.

Had the Lord really directed me to do this? Faith seemed to be just beyond my grasp. *Oh Father, help my unbelief.* I persisted in speaking and affirming God's Word, returning it to Him in the form of prayer. Then one evening I was led to three verses that seemed to leap off the pages of the Bible.

"My Word does not return to Me empty, but accomplishes and achieves the purpose for which I sent it."[7] "I am watching to see that My Word is performed."[8] "God gives life to the dead and refers to things that are not yet in existence as though they already were."[9]

I believed the Lord was speaking directly to me. Faith exploded in my heart, and I knew I was healed. No, the symptoms didn't disappear. Yet I was sure God would make evident the healing in my body in His perfect timing.

My situation remained unchanged for another four months. That time seemed to pass rapidly, although everything continued to whirl dizzily around me. It didn't matter. I had found my hiding place in this storm and was overcoming my circumstances by faith and trust in God. Fully persuaded that God was performing His Word in me,[10] I found that the vapor of my depression vanished.

In early February 1996, nearly one year from the onslaught of the first vertigo attack, it happened. As I leaned into a closet, the violent spinning and reeling ceased abruptly. There are no words adequate to express the joy of experiencing that stillness. It was as if the dark clouds parted and the sun burst forth.

I braced one hand against the closet floor to remain steady, not wanting any motion to disturb the stillness. Bent over in that ridiculous posture, I heard His voice, "Rejoice." Slowly I inched my way to a standing position, leaning against a wall for support. Nothing reeled. Tears of joy gushed to my eyes, and I began praising the Lord. Again I heard, "Rejoice."

I had once read that the literal translation of the Hebrew word translated in the Bible as "rejoice" is to twirl about, like a calf kicking up his heels after being released from a stall. *Does the Lord really want me to start twirling—on purpose? What if the vertigo returns?* With some hesitation at first, I began circling and singing His praises.

A verse came streaming into my mind: " 'The LORD your God is with you, he is mighty to save. He will take great delight in you, he will quiet you with his love, he will rejoice over you with singing.' "[11] I like to think that as the angels watched on that day, they saw the Lord and me joyously celebrating together.

> " 'The LORD your God is with you, he is mighty to save. He will take great delight in you, he will quiet you with his love, he will rejoice over you with singing' "
>
> (Zephaniah 3:17, NIV).

Reflecting on the year of my vertigo, I know this—only by the grace of God did I weather the worst physical and mental storm of my life. The transforming power of His Word restored my hope. God's promises became the anchor for my soul[12] and kept me from being double-minded. When I placed my trust in Him and His ability to perform His Word, He placed me in an ark called "Hope" and brought me into a

> *From the depths of depression, He brought me into a new relationship with His Word. There He showed me He had a plan for my life, and it was better than the one I was living.*

calm place—the eye of the hurricane. There the God of peace[13] rode out the storm with me.

God had to allow me to reach the brink of despair to convince me of my need to rely totally on Him. From the depths of depression, He brought me into a new relationship with His Word. There He showed me He had a plan for my life, and it was better than the one I was living. He opened a door of understanding, inviting me to trust and experience His great love. **God became the object of my faith.** Trust in His ability to perform His Word became my sure foundation.

I have treasured the words of His mouth
More than my necessary food
(Job 23:12, NKJV).

Bless Job's heart. This statement shows he was a man who knew the true Source of life.

Like Job, I appreciate my desperate need for the Word of God. My life depends on it—His Word is life to me.

References

1. Deuteronomy 32:47, paraphrased.
2. 1 Kings 19:12.
3. Deuteronomy 30:19.
4. 2 Corinthians 10:5.
5. Romans 10:17.
6. Habakkuk 2:2, NKJV.
7. Isaiah 55:11, paraphrased.
8. Jeremiah 1:12, paraphrased.
9. Romans 4:17, paraphrased.
10. Romans 4:21.
11. Zephaniah 3:17, NIV.
12. Hebrews 6:19.
13. Philippians 4:9.

Chapter Three
How God Raised Up a Word Warrior

Weeks after the Lord healed me, I returned to Houston on a business trip. I was eager to visit my old church, and my arrival was timed perfectly for a great blessing. A three-day revival was just starting—I could attend each evening. The services were lengthy, but the Bible study was so anointed I didn't want the preacher to stop. Being with old friends and hearing inspiring messages was like a taste of heaven.

On the last evening, the music service was particularly special. As prayers of worship ascended on wings of musical notes, a profound reverence settled over the congregation. We were pressing into that deep place of unhurried worship in song. The presence of the Lord was almost tangible. As I often do during songs of heartfelt worship, I closed my eyes to focus on God and shut out all distractions. But something caused me to look up and notice a young man on the worship team. From his closed eyes and the slight upward tilt of his face, I sensed he was singing for an audience of One—a sincere prayer to the God of his life. It was precious to see.

The song service achieved its purpose—hearts were softened and opened to receive God's Word. A dynamic study on God's faithfulness followed. At the close of the meeting, I walked out of the building beside the young man from the worship team. I asked how he was doing and was flabbergasted at his negative reply. How could despair overcome him so quickly after pressing into God's presence in song and in the Word?

Returning to my hotel room, I sought God for the answer. Why do Christians lose their victory? Why is it we can "cross over" to the Land of Promise when we're behind church walls, worship in spirit and in truth, echo "amen" to the teaching— only to return to an attitude of defeat and discouragement when we leave the building? I wasn't finger-pointing. This young man wasn't the only example I had in mind. I realized most of us suffer from this syndrome. God directed me to the Old Testament for the answer.

Giants in the land

When the Lord sent Moses to rescue the Israelites from Egyptian bondage, He promised to give them possession of a "land flowing with milk and honey."[1] Today, we refer to this as the Promised Land. Bible history records the many miracles God performed during the deliverance of His people. As He led them out of Egypt and through the desert, His Presence went with them.[2] He sustained them every step of the way to the borders of the Promised Land.

Standing at the edge of promise, they were instructed to "go in and possess" the land God had set before them.[3] This land was theirs, given by His solemn vow. Although Moses told them to advance without fear, the Israelites would not accept this counsel. Rather than going forward on the word of God, the community felt it would be wiser to test the way of entry. They suggested that a group of spies be sent in first.[4] God agreed to their request and instructed Moses to select one leader from each tribe to serve on the team of scouts.[5]

God's word of promise was of no value to them, because they did not combine the message of God with faith.

The rest is history. The twelve spies entered the Promised Land, and upon their return all agreed on one thing: "Surely it flows with milk and honey."[6] Still, the differences in their reports marked the dividing line between the faithless and the faithful. Ten of the scouts were fearful and discouraged. Their eyes had beheld the inhabitants of this land as giants, and, in comparison, they felt as mere grasshoppers.[7] The report from the ten faithless spies forecasted doom and defeat.

Meanwhile, two of the scouts—Joshua and Caleb—held fast to God's promise. On the authority of His word, they said the land could be conquered and possessed by the power of God. Their attitude was, If God is with us, who can stand against us? Joshua and Caleb confidently advised the people to go up and claim their possession.[8]

Which report did the Israelite camp believe and receive? The message of God's faithfulness to His promise, or the report of faithless men? The entire camp heard and reacted to one thing—**there are giants in the land!** God's word of promise was of no value to them, because they did not combine the message of God with faith.[9]

With their own eyes, they had witnessed God's wondrous works throughout their journey. Yet they still did not trust Him to keep His vows to them. Sounds of weeping, murmuring, and complaining filled the camp. The Israelites brazenly refused to receive the testimony of God. Because of their sin of unbelief, God sentenced them to wander around the desert for forty years, until the adult generation passed away. Lack of faith literally shut them out of the Promised Land.

It's amazing how faithless the people of God could be in Bible times. And we still are today. We hear God's Word and become enthusiastic in the hearing. But when we look at the obstacles of life, we cry out, "There are giants in the land!" Suffering from the "grasshopper identity syndrome," we wring our hands with worry. Doubt and disbelief get a stranglehold on our hearts and choke off the life of God's promises. God's message is of no value to us unless we combine our faith with His Word. God's promises are ushered into existence through faith.

> *Doubt and disbelief get a stranglehold on our hearts and choke off the life of God's promises.*

As I studied in my hotel room, God made something very clear to me. Without faith, I cannot please Him. This lesson should be a serious warning to all of us. When we doubt God's promises, we doubt His testimony. And when we doubt His testimony, we regard Him as a liar.

> Anyone who does not believe God has made him out to be a liar,
> because he has not believed the testimony God has given
> *(1 John 5:10, NIV).*

No wonder it's impossible to please God without faith.[10] When we don't believe God, we are disobeying Him—just like the Israelites in the desert. Unbelief is a sin that keeps us from entering into God's promises.[11]

Understanding this brought me to my knees, repenting before the Lord. He had demonstrated that His Word is life to me. He had proven that His thoughts were higher than I could comprehend.[12] I had been growing in "Word power," but I knew I had not entered the dimension of faith that He desired for me. I recalled the many Scriptures that assure us His vows are for us. The Bible says God performs all things on our behalf.[13]

Life affirmations from Scripture

I asked the Lord to show me what to do. The Holy Spirit kept me up the rest of the night, flooding my heart with Scripture.[14] It seemed that every verse I'd ever heard in my life was brought to my remembrance. The Spirit led me to write these promises of God, His vows, in the form of affirmations beginning with the words, "I am." I was to speak these—just as I had spoken God's healing promises. Faith would come by hearing.[15] God knew I needed to hear the testimony of my own voice.

By morning, I had recorded over one hundred affirmations, compiled from possibly five times as many Scriptures. I spent a day thumbing through my Bible and located nearly half the references, but I had no idea where to look for the others. Some of what I had written sounded so unfamiliar, I wondered if they were even Bible verses. It required a visit to the church library and a great effort in *Strong's Concordance* to identify the remaining Scriptures. I was elated to find them all. The church secretary let me use her computer to type the affirmations, and I made sure the pastor received a copy before I left town.

God began a great work in my life through the practice of affirming His Word—a work that continues to grow—and not in me alone. Several weeks after I returned home, an elder from the Houston church phoned. Evidently, the pastor mentioned that someone had given him affirmations from Scripture, and the elder guessed I was the one. What thrilled my heart, though, was that the pastor had told the congregation that God was changing his life through the affirmations.

This pastor was an accomplished student of the Bible. I feel certain he was familiar with all the supporting Scriptures. Yet, like me, he tapped into a new source of transforming power in the affirmation practice. He never called me with this testimony. He knew that God deserved all the glory.[16] I recognized that, as well.

It was 1996 when the Lord first raised me up as a "Word Warrior." For the next two years, He worked through me in ministry outreach. Then I returned to the corporate world for eighteen months, and a frenzied schedule consumed the priority of God's Word. And, you guessed it, my backsliding began to distance me from the Lord. I was miserable, in spite of great career success. But God led me back to affirming His Word in September 1999, and resuming this practice brought an incredible revelation.

Immediately when I returned to speaking God's Word and affirming His promises, there was a surge in the power and victory of my Christian walk.

Immediately when I returned to speaking God's Word and affirming His promises, there was a surge in the power and victory of my Christian walk. *A power really exists in this process,* I shouted inwardly. *Teach me, Lord, to understand why, so I can teach others this marvelous truth.*

God often performs a work in me that develops without my awareness. Usually I enjoy the benefits for a while before recognizing He has changed me. But this was different. It was immediately obvious I had been "endued with power from on high."[17] The intimacy of my relationship with Christ had been instantly restored. He was my "First Love" again.[18] Seeking Him first in all things was my earnest desire.[19] Doing His will was my top priority. I realized the transformation came through the process of affirming His Word. I just didn't understand why that process worked so powerfully.

"Set up road signs; put up guideposts. Take note of the highway, the road that you take."[20] God has taught me to seek Him for understanding when He has done a work in me. His ways are superior to our ways. I'm not satisfied just to enjoy a higher level of experiencing God—I want to know how He transported me there. Understanding His leading helps me to set up signposts on His holy highway. These markers are critical to me. Not merely because I want to direct others, but also to help me identify the way back if I ever step off the narrow path.

A ministry is born

After several weeks of intense study, I came to understand the mystery of the power of affirming His Word with my living voice. I felt compelled to share the affirmations with others. I self-published *Life Affirmations from Scripture* and distributed free copies to dozens of ministries and over a hundred individuals. The moving testimonies I received later reconfirmed the spiritual power of the affirmation practice.

One month later, January 2000, I accepted God's call to full-time ministry. Word Warrior Ministries was birthed by God's leading. I've never advertised or promoted this ministry. The Lord has provided all my assignments, opening amazing avenues from the very beginning. The Holy Spirit impressed me that doors for television, radio, and publishing would open wide and that I would speak to nations around the world. I was astonished, but I didn't doubt Him. I confess to thinking, *Who am I that You would use me in this way?* The Lord caused me to understand this: **It's all about Him—and not about me.**

On December 31, 2002, I made my first guest appearance on Three Angels Broadcasting Network (3ABN), a Christian television station that reaches every continent on earth. (There's an amusing irony in this, which I'll share later, toward the last of the book.) Seated with Danny Shelton, 3ABN's president, I reflected in amazement on God's faithfulness to His Word. By the grace of God, I welcomed the New Year sharing a Bible teaching with the world. Amazing! Six weeks later, I was overjoyed for a second opportunity to share another message on the network.

Then a few months passed, and 3ABN invited me to host a new series and to write a program companion book. My "miracle" assignment had really arrived. At the time I lived in a small, rural Texas community of about five thousand people. A person would have to be dreaming to think such a weighty assignment could find its way to me there, right? Yet I knew it would. The mission came sooner than expected and was greater than anticipated. Still, by faith, I did eagerly expect it.[21] As long as I keep exalting His Word, I know the Lord will continue to provide ears to hear.

> *God wants to raise up many Word warriors—a multitude of voices exalting His Word.*

God called me, through 3ABN, to write my experience for your benefit. To set your heart toward His highway and give you landmarks and signposts that will point you in the right direction. To inform you of His power source made available to you—a power that will produce an abundant life and godliness.[22]

God wants to raise up many Word warriors—a multitude of voices exalting His Word. My earnest prayer is that this book will inspire you to give the Lord permission to have His way with you through the creative power of His Word. If you will, I have absolute confidence that you'll never regret it.

To God be the glory!

References

1. Exodus 3:6–10.
2. Exodus 33:14.
3. Deuteronomy 1:8, 21.
4. Deuteronomy 1:21–26.
5. Numbers 13:1, 2.
6. Numbers 13:27.
7. Numbers 13:33.
8. Numbers 13:30; 14:6–9.
9. Hebrews 4:2.
10. Hebrews 11:6.
11. Hebrews 3:19.
12. Isaiah 55:9.
13. Psalm 57:2.
14. John 14:26.
15. Romans 10:17.
16. Isaiah 48:11.
17. Luke 24:49, NKJV.
18. Revelation 2:4.
19. Matthew 6:33.
20. Jeremiah 31:21, NIV.
21. Hebrews 11:1.
22. John 10:10.

Section Two

Victory for the Church

Chapter Four
The Identity Crisis

While standing in his wheat field, a farmer and his banker talked about their ministry efforts for Christ. The banker, dressed in a three-pieced suit, said, "I have an anointing from the Lord." Outfitted in bib overalls, the farmer glanced down and began digging the toe of his boot into the soil, "Oh mercy, I love the Lord, and I serve Him with all my heart, but I wouldn't dare say that I'm anointed."

Which of these men acted in humility? Christ was the anointed One of God, filled with power from on high. Wasn't the banker boasting when he claimed that same anointing? Aren't we naturally drawn to the simple self-abasing attitude of the farmer?

I often use this story in churches to illustrate our upside-down thinking. When I invite audiences to vote for which man is the example of true humility, nearly all choose the farmer. Most people instantly dismiss the banker as a hypocrite, perhaps because this story reminds us of the Pharisee and the tax collector.

The Bible account of two men praying in the temple is recorded in the Gospel of Luke, chapter eighteen.[1] A pompous Pharisee stood thanking God that he wasn't like other sinners and began listing the deeds of his religious performance. His judgmental attitude flowed from a spirit of self-righteousness. His opinion of himself contradicted God's truth. We're all sinners in need of a Savior,[2] and we're warned not to compare ourselves to others.[3]

In contrast, the tax collector begged for God's mercy, beating his breast and confessing his sin. His act of humility agreed with the counsel of God's Word.[4] Can we compare the actions of these two men to the banker and the farmer? Yes, I think we can. But the results might surprise you. We must look first at God's testimony of who we are in Christ.

> The anointing which you have received from Him abides in you . . .
> the same anointing teaches you concerning all things, and is true,
> and is not a lie,
> and just as it has taught you, you will abide in Him.
> *(1 John 2:27, NKJV).*

> *Our act of humility is to accept God's testimony and not depend on our own reasoning. We must cast down every vain argument—every thought and opinion that proudly exalts itself above the Word of God.*

That's God's declaration about **all** who are abiding in Christ. Our act of humility is to accept God's testimony and not depend on our own reasoning.[5] We must cast down every vain argument—every thought and opinion that proudly exalts itself above the Word of God.[6] Our experiences may be our reality, but that doesn't make them "truth." Truth is measured by only one standard—the Holy Bible of God.[7]

If both the banker and the farmer of my imaginary scene were abiding in Christ, the Lord would endorse the banker as the humble speaking man. Why? By affirming that he had an anointing, the banker revealed that he believed—and humbly accepted—God's testimony. While the farmer thought he was being humble, he exalted his opinion over the Word of God. He spoke either from ignorance or from a refusal to accept what the Bible teaches about his identity in Christ.

Our lesson is this—even if we don't *feel* anointed, we must agree that we are if God tells us it is so. We can't operate by feelings. They are often the defective product of warped human reasoning. Doubting God's Word is the essence of pride. Since the beginning of time, Satan has used the device of "doubt and disbelief" to trap us in sin.[8]

Christians are suffering from an identity crisis. We're walking in error because we don't know the Scriptures or the power of God.[9] Our quality of life is destroyed from lack of knowledge[10] on two critical matters:

- We don't understand God's plan for our lives.
- We have little awareness of who we are "in Christ."

For some, the crisis of identity results from a shameful neglect of Bible study. We live in a generation that seeks quick escape hatches from the stresses of our world.

Entertainment has been elevated to idolatry. Many sacrifice great chunks of time at the altar of this coveted idol. Christians aren't immune to this practice. We can make many excuses to sit mindlessly in front of the television for hours. *I need*

THE IDENTITY CRISIS

Chapter 4

to relax. I deserve a break. My family is doing it, and I should stay in the room with them. It's easy to become satisfied with a meager effort in Bible study. Apathy is a dangerous heart condition.

On the other hand, there's a second group of us who are devoted to Bible study, yet still walk in the darkness of mistaken identity. Our hearts don't overflow with love, joy, and peace. We aren't stirred to activity by the zeal of the Holy Spirit. We're impotent instead of powerful—and we can't figure out why. Fearing others would judge us harshly, we hide our condition. What we don't realize is that the same snare has entrapped most Christians.

> *Christians are suffering from an identity crisis. We're walking in error because we don't know the Scriptures or the power of God.*

Countless souls have approached me with tears regarding this testimony. They seem to feel a certain ease in sharing with me, maybe because I minister by example, telling of my past failures and giving God the glory for the power to change. On the other hand, it might be simply because I'm from out of town, and they figure their secret is stored at a safe distance when I leave.

A "heart cry" answered—the vision in the mirror

Christians cry out for the answer to their crises of identity. Many years ago, that was my heart cry, and I asked the Lord to help me understand. The answer came from the Bible: "But be doers of the word, and not hearers only, deceiving yourselves. For if anyone is a hearer of the word and not a doer, he is like a man observing his natural face in a mirror; for he observes himself, goes away, and immediately forgets what kind of man he was. But he who looks into the perfect law of liberty and continues *in it,* and is not a forgetful hearer but a doer of the work, this one will be blessed in what he does" (James 1:22–25, NKJV).

Here we're told that when we read the Word of God, we see a vision, a reflection, of who we are "in Christ." The Word reveals a mirror image of our re-created "born-again" nature. We read the wonderful promises and observe the image of our new nature, but, laying our Bibles aside, we immediately forget what we look like. We lose the vision of God's promises to us, and—without a vision—the promises perish. We become **hearers** of the Word and not **doers.**

3—E. H. W.

33

> *We lose the vision of God's promises to us, and—without a vision—the promises perish.*

Jesus said, "Blessed—happy and to be envied—rather are they who hear the Word of God and obey *and* practice it!"[11] It's true, some simply don't put God's Word into practice because it requires effort, and they're lazy. But I believe that most of us don't walk in God's promises because we can't wrap our mind around the concepts. It seems impossible to apply such lofty statements to ourselves. *Me? I have an anointing from God?* Focusing on our weakness instead of on the power of God, we struggle with obedience. Our Christian experience is lackluster and without joy.

Void of God's power,[12] we slip into a performance of external religious practices. Then guilt and condemnation come knocking at the door. We stumble, strive to get back on our feet, tidy our outward appearance, and put up a good front for others to see. *Oh, what's wrong with me, Lord? No one else seems to have these problems. How can You love me when I keep failing You?* We sometimes feel so unworthy to receive God's love.

Set your heart at ease. God demonstrated His amazing love by sending Christ to die for you. You are worth much to the Lord. You are a special treasure to Him. Before you ever knew Him, God paid your ransom—the price to redeem and deliver you from the bondage of sin. You are worth nothing less than the price He paid for you. It cost Him the precious lifeblood of His Son, Jesus Christ.[13] That's how much you're worth to God.

> *You are worth nothing less than the price He paid for you. It cost Him the precious lifeblood of His Son, Jesus Christ.*

Put your memories to rest. Is there some sin you've asked God to forgive repeatedly, yet the memory of it keeps coming back to haunt you? If you have sincerely repented and confessed your sin to the Lord, He has forgiven you. Not only has He forgiven you, He has also cleansed your record of all unrighteousness.[14] Accept that God's ways are higher than ours. Quit trying to limit His ability to forgive and forget. When God forgives our confessed sins, He remembers them no more.[15] In loving mercy, He removes our sins as "far as the east is from the west."[16]

Blessed is he whose transgression is forgiven,
Whose sin is covered.
Blessed is the man to whom the LORD does not impute iniquity,
And in whose spirit there is no guile. . . .
I acknowledged my sin to You,
And my iniquity I have not hidden.
I said,
"I will confess my transgressions to the LORD,"
And You forgave the iniquity of my sin.
For this cause everyone who is godly shall pray to You
In a time when You may be found
(Psalm 32:1–2, 5, 6, NKJV).

If you have difficulty accepting God's forgiveness, consider what the Lord had to say about David after his death. God instructed a prophet to deliver this message to the wicked King Jeroboam, "You have not been as My servant David, who kept My commandments and who followed Me with all his heart, to do only what was right in My eyes."[17] This Scripture vividly proves this point: ***God forgot what David asked Him to forgive.***

King David had a heart for God, but he certainly broke God's commandments and did evil. Then David humbled himself and repented of his sins in sincere love for the Lord. The fifty-first psalm is the tender record of David's plea for forgiveness and a marvelous lesson in the joy of repentance. In my Bible, I've made a note at Psalm 51 to refer me to God's account, in 1 Kings 14:8, of David's clean record after he repented. I always want to remember that—Hallelujah!— the outcome of our confession of sin is that **God forgets what we ask Him to forgive!**

The message to King Jeroboam, represented as the very words of God, causes me to rejoice for another reason. If we want proof that the Bible is divinely inspired, I think this is a wonderful example. The writer of this account must have been under the inspiration of the Holy Spirit. Any human agent presuming to write for God would have recorded something like this: "You've not been as David, who after he committed adultery and was guilty of murder, confessed his sin and repented. But, *after* I forgave him, David did what was right in My eyes for the rest of his life."

Don't you agree that's the only reasoning a human mind could produce? By God's grace, we've been given the ability to forgive others, but we lack the capacity to wipe away all memory of our acts of forgiveness. In fact, we're amazed to think God can actually forget our sins.

> Let us therefore come boldly to the throne of grace,
> that we may obtain mercy and find grace to help in time of need. . . .
> "For I will be merciful to their unrighteousness,
> and their sins and their lawless deeds I will remember no more"
> *(Hebrews 4:16; 8:12, NKJV).*

Useless religion

Returning to our study of James 1:22–25 where we're told that God's Word reflects our new nature, we find an interesting contrast. James speaks of the hope found in abiding in the "perfect law of liberty." We'll study this wonderful law in depth in the next chapter. When that law is at work within us, James says we'll be blessed in the practice of God's Word. In stark contrast, he continues in verse 26 speaking out against worthless religion. He says if we don't bridle our tongue, help the needy, and keep ourselves from being polluted by evil, our religion is useless.

Is it possible we could be regular churchgoers, class teachers, possibly even ministers of the gospel, and yet be practicing useless religion?

"Useless religion"—what a thought-provoking concept! Examining our Bibles, we can find many examples of worthless religious practices. Is it possible we could be regular churchgoers, class teachers, possibly even ministers of the gospel, and yet be practicing useless religion?

This introduces a third category of professing Christians who suffer an identity crisis. The cause for their condition is chasing after the doctrines of men rather than seeking the Word of God. Jesus said if we follow the commandments and traditions of men, we make God's Word of no effect—we've illegally emptied God's Word of His lawful authority.[18]

Unlawful teachings of men are developed when any of these practices occur:

- Doctrines are "distorted truths" based on Scripture taken out of context, rather than on the related teachings of the entire Bible.
- Humans interpret symbolic language from outside sources rather than allowing the Bible to interpret itself, Scripture upon Scripture.
- A religious system has arrogantly assumed authority to change God's eternal Word.

> This people honors Me with their lips,
> but their heart is far from Me. And in vain they worship Me,
> Teaching as doctrines the commandments of men
> *(Mark 7:6, 7, NKJV).*

Doctrines of men can be so wildly developed they become useless religion. I don't believe that walking in "unknown error" automatically qualifies us as worshiping in vain. If that were true, we'd all be in trouble. None of us has yet to receive all of God's truth. The Bible tells us that the path of the righteous will grow brighter and brighter until the coming of Jesus.[19] The entrance of His Word brings increased light and understanding.[20]

The Bible tells us the path of the righteous will grow brighter and brighter until the coming of Jesus. The entrance of His Word brings increased light and understanding.

God is merciful and looks at the intent of our hearts.[21] The name of the church we attend is not the basis for salvation. I believe the Bible teaches that many sincere seekers of God have received the gift of eternal life, but are still walking in error. Based on Revelation 18:4, where the voice from heaven calls God's people out of spiritual Babylon, I believe God has His people in every denomination today. Still, it's critical to heed the call to come out of error. We must study the Bible for ourselves and see if what we've been taught is truly the commandment of God.

The best advice my mother ever gave me was, "Don't accept what you hear from the pulpit just because a preacher says it's true. Get into the Bible and check it out for yourself." When the Lord led me to follow this advice, I was shocked to find I had been defending and holding fast to some grievous errors.

Jesus said we could know who belongs to Him by the fruits they bear.[22] Fruit only comes by union. If we're grafted into Jesus,[23] the true Vine, our fruit (actions) will be of His Spirit. Still, to ensure we aren't fooled by counterfeits, the Bible instructs us to put all things to the test and to hold fast only to what is good.[24] It's possible that the outward appearance of fruit can be deceitful.

While visiting a friend's home recently, my empty stomach was growling. Spotting a bowl of shiny red apples on her table, my mouth began to water. I asked her permission and grabbed one for a snack. Although it looked as authentic as the real thing, it had a strange feeling. Examining it more carefully and hearing my friend's laughter, I realized I'd been duped by appearance—fruit appealing to the eye, but artificial. Likewise, there are practices that may appeal to our senses as fruits of His Spirit, but we must examine everything in the light of His Word to see if they stand the test of truth.

> *Any religious practice that doesn't line up with God's commandments and counsel is useless.*

What, then, is useless religion? As we've just reviewed, any religious practice that doesn't line up with God's commandments and counsel is useless. Still another useless practice is if our religious observance is merely external. Consider the life of the Pharisees. External religion relies on "self performance" and does not recognize the need of developing and depending on a living relationship with a perfect Savior. We can't work our way to heaven.[25] We become children of God only by relationship, and only His children will enter the heavenly Jerusalem.[26]

What about those who think they are in relationship with the Lord? Does the potential exist to be deceived about eternal security? What does Jesus say?

> "Not everyone who says to Me, 'Lord, Lord,' shall enter the kingdom of heaven, but he who **does the will** of My Father in heaven. Many will say to Me in that day, 'Lord, Lord, have we not prophesied in Your name, cast out demons in Your name, and done many wonders in Your name?' And then I will declare to them, 'I never knew you; depart from Me, you who **practice lawlessness!**'"
> *(Matthew 7:20–23, NKJV).*

Please note the two patterns of behavior Christ is contrasting in this text. He says the one who "does the will of My Father" will enter the kingdom of heaven. But He rejects those who "practice lawlessness."

Unfortunately, some Bibles translate the word *lawlessness* as "evil." That makes me wonder: *Will those who receive Christ's stinging indictment think they had been practicing evil in His name?* Other translators have chosen the word "iniquity," but the most accurate translation of the Greek word found in this text is "lawlessness."

> Whoever commits sin also commits lawlessness, and sin is lawlessness
> *(1 John 3:4, NKJV).*

According to the Bible, the **definition of sin is lawlessness**—the breaking of the law of God; the ignoring of His divine government.

Those who will say, "Lord, Lord, have we not done many wonders in your name," evidently had no genuine love for God. Jesus said if we loved Him, we would keep His commandments.[27] This group, who broke His commandments while professing to know Him, is defined as liars by the Bible:

> Now by this we know that we know Him, if we keep His commandments.
> He who says, "I know Him," and does not keep His commandments,
> is a **liar,** and the truth is not in him
> *(1 John 2:3, 4, NKJV).*

Christ rejects this group because they have not been born again of His Spirit, living in union with Him, and—by His power—doing the will of His Father. The Bible is clear that if they had been born of God, they would have obeyed.[28]

This doesn't mean God's children are without sin, but that our love motivates us to please our Lord. His Spirit within us will prevent us from walking in the continuous practice of disobedience. We're quick to recognize when we're not walking in Christ's footsteps and even quicker to repent. And nothing can separate us from His love.[29]

"He is also able to save to the uttermost those who come to God through Him, since He always lives to make intercession for them"

(Hebrews 7:25, NKJV).

Our loving Savior will not reject a child of His. On the contrary, "He is also able to save to the uttermost those who come to God through Him, since He always lives to make intercession for them."[30]

Following the light of His Word

To overcome useless religion, we must always seek a balanced teaching from God's Word. For example, the Bible clearly teaches we're made righteous by faith in Christ.[31] Righteousness by faith is the only kind of righteousness there is.[32] Though this is true, the Bible also says that when we've received the righteousness of Christ in our hearts, we'll be empowered to practice righteousness.[33] We're not trying to earn salvation. The desire and power to follow God's teaching flows naturally from our born-again hearts.

Salvation is a gift from God. We're saved by grace, through faith in Christ.[34] There's nothing we can do to save ourselves, but that doesn't release us from obedience. When Christ was on earth, He didn't obey God to *become* the Son of God—He obeyed His Father because He *was* the Son of God. Likewise, we don't obey God *to be* saved—we obey because we *are* saved. The Holy Spirit empowers us to walk in obedience to God's truth.

Obedience is the pathway to God's blessing and the highest expression of our worship of Him. Christ is the Source of eternal salvation for all those who walk in obedience to Him. This is not my opinion—I have it on the authority of God's Word:

He became the author of eternal salvation to all who **obey** Him
(Hebrews 5:9, NKJV).

God's people are suffering from an identity crisis. The symptoms vary and might be mental anguish, lukewarm indifference, or stony cold hearts. This identity crisis is the greatest problem in the Christian community today. Now that's a bold statement.

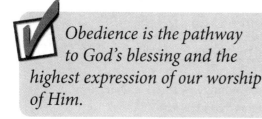

Obedience is the pathway to God's blessing and the highest expression of our worship of Him.

It causes me to pause and think I should water it down with some little qualifier, like "one of the greatest" problems, or "in my opinion." *Why is it so great a problem?* Human reasoning demands the answer. Unless we recognize this barrier for what it is, it will continue to block our advancement.

Ignorance (not knowing), or **ignore**-*ance* (knowing, but neglecting), of God's Word is the root of the problem. If we don't know God's plan, we don't understand who we have become when we are included "in Christ."[35] This prevents us from walking in the grace of God. It repels the heavenly love, light, life, and power. Living in the kingdom of His marvelous light is not a matter of talking the talk, but it is the power to walk in His footsteps along the path of life.[36]

Still I had to ask: *Lord, am I making an overstatement by saying our identity crisis is our greatest problem?* It's funny how we can know something, but not know that we know. God had given me the answer before I asked the question. In fact, I wrote about it in chapter three. Do you remember?

An identity crisis is what kept the Israelites from entering the Promised Land. They wouldn't accept God's plan for their lives. They couldn't appreciate who they were as His chosen people. The crisis of identity kept them from mixing faith with the message of God, and they had to wander around the desert until they died. Doubt and disbelief in His Word were the sins that kept them from entering His promises.[37] Do we want to repeat their mistake?

> *Our loving Savior is calling us out of darkness and into the Land of Promise. He will turn all of our obstacles into steppingstones, as we follow the light of His Word.*

Praise God, there is a way to overcome the identity crisis! We'll find it by knowing the Scriptures and experiencing the power of God that is available to us. We must understand God's plan for our lives and learn who we are "in Christ." Motivated by love and empowered by God, we will find His commandments become a joy to follow as part of His loving plan. Because of our faith in Christ and His conquering power at work within us, we become victorious over the polluted ways of the world system.

> For this is the love of God, that we keep His commandments.
> And His commandments are not burdensome.
> For whatever is born of God overcomes the world.
> And this is the victory that has overcome the world—our faith.
> Who is he who overcomes the world,
> but he who believes that Jesus is the Son of God?
> *(1 John 5:3–5, NKJV).*

God is drawing us closer to Him and away from useless religion. In the dark, we can't find our way or see the reflection of our new image. Our loving Savior is calling us out of darkness and into the Land of Promise. He will turn all of our obstacles into steppingstones as we follow the light of His Word. Walking in the power of His promises, we will overcome our identity crisis.

References

1. Luke 18:10–14.
2. Romans 3:23.
3. Luke 6:37.
4. 1 John 1:9.
5. Proverbs 3:5.
6. 2 Corinthians 10:5.
7. John 17:17.
8. Genesis 3:1.
9. Matthew 22:29.
10. Hosea 4:6.
11. Luke 11:28, AMP.
12. 2 Timothy 3:5.
13. 1 Peter 1:18, 19.
14. 1 John 1:9.
15. Jeremiah 31:34.
16. Psalm 103:12.
17. 1 Kings 14:8, NKJV.
18. Mark 7:13.
19. Proverbs 4:18.
20. Psalm 119:130.
21. 1 Samuel 16:7.
22. Matthew 7:16, 20.
23. Romans 11:24.
24. 1 Thessalonians 5:21.
25. Ephesians 2:8, 9.
26. Revelation 3:12; 21:2.
27. John 14:15.
28. 1 John 2:29; 3:7–14.
29. Romans 8:38, 39.
30. Hebrews 7:25, NKJV.
31. 2 Corinthians 5:21.
32. Isaiah 64:6.
33. 1 John 3:7.
34. Ephesians 2:8–10.
35. 1 Corinthians 1:30.
36. 1 John 2:6.
37. Hebrews 3:19.

Chapter Five
Overcoming the Identity Crisis

Where is the God of Moses, who parted the Red Sea?[1] Where is the God of Joshua, who made the sun stand still?[2] Where is the God of Peter, who bestowed so much power that the casting of the apostle's shadow healed the sick?[3] Have you ever been tempted to ask questions like these? We've got it backwards when we think like that. God declares He is the same yesterday, today, and forever. "I am the Lord; I change not."[4]

Let's reverse our thinking. Where are His children who believe God has miracle-working power to deliver them? Where are His people who look to God to do what seems impossible in the physical realm? Where are His followers who walk so closely in step with the Spirit that the casting of their shadow heals? The healing power of the Holy Spirit flowed through Peter's shadow. "He who is joined to the Lord is one spirit *with Him*."[5] So the silhouette Peter cast was a shadow united as one with Him.

What can we conclude about these men of the Bible?

- They understood God's plan, because His Word was in their hearts.
- They assumed a new identity in Him.
- Because they had overcome their identity crises, God could trust them with His power.

Wouldn't it be wonderful if God had outlined eight steps to end the dark days of our identity crisis? One, two, three . . . eight, and it's done! In truth, it wouldn't be wonderful at all. If it were that simple, we wouldn't earnestly seek Him. Our self-absorbed natures would become satisfied with some mechanical routine focused on performance, rather than on relationship. Human reasoning would convince us those few steps were all we needed to know.

Instead, God designed a plan—a series of interlocking systems of truths—for us to achieve victory in identity. Our Lord is a God of order. He is very "system oriented" and wants to guide our every step to success. If we practice His principles, truth will explode every myth and misconception we have.

Every word that the Spirit inspired men to record reveals to us the character of God, His loving plan, and our passage to a new identity.

What I would like to share with you is *everything* the Holy Spirit has taught me about overcoming my identity crisis. In fact, I would write a book on this if it hadn't already been written. Most likely, you have the Book on your night table or desk or on a shelf somewhere. It's the Bible. Every word that the Spirit inspired men to record reveals to us the character of God, His loving plan, and our passage to a new identity.

My journey has required much study. I'm not suggesting that I've completely recovered from the identity crisis, but I've come a long way. I would *like* to share everything He has taught me, but I can't. What I *will* share are a few of the guideposts, or road signs, the Lord used to direct me toward a better understanding.

Glimpses of grace

Grace revealed His goodness and caused me to embrace His Word as my daily requirement for spiritual strength and growth. Here are glimpses of grace that stirred my heart to search for the new identity God offered me:

- God has a brilliant plan for my life, and I can read all about it in the Bible. *Jeremiah 29:11.*
- God's Word is life to me, my spiritual nutrition. *Deuteronomy 32:46, 47; Matthew 4:4.*
- Abiding in His Word gives me the mind of Christ. *1 Corinthians 2:16.*
- God knows the end from the beginning, works everything in agreement with His plan, and counts everything as completed (even things not yet accomplished in my sight). *Isaiah 46:10; Ephesians 1:11; Romans 4:17.*
- I can know the end from the beginning because "it is written," and God watches over His Word to perform it. *Isaiah 46:10; Jeremiah 1:12.*
- He wants me to trust Him, leaning on His Word rather than on my own understanding. He wants me to acknowledge that His ways are better than my ways. *Proverbs 3:5, 6.*
- God wants me to depend totally on Him. He will empower me to do everything He asks of me. He will **cause** me to be all that He has **called** me to

be. Dependence upon Him is the "law of liberty." *Philippians 2:13; Hebrews 13:20, 21; Philippians 1:6; James 1:25.*

- I am included "in Christ." *1 Corinthians 1:30.*
- Everything God does in my life is for my **eternal** benefit; my destiny is to be conformed to the image of His Son, day by day. *Romans 8:28, 29; 2 Corinthians 3:18.*
- All of His promises are mine—here and now—if I pursue His ways. *2 Corinthians 1:20.*
- I partake of the divine nature by partaking of His promises. *2 Peter 1:3, 4.*
- I am who God says I am. *2 Corinthians 5:17; 1 Corinthians 15:10.*
- Obedience is the pathway to blessing. *Hebrews 10:36; James 1:25.*

It's overly ambitious to think that all these wonderful truths can be addressed in a single chapter. The experiences God has led me through in each of these points of His grace could fill volumes. The best I can hope to accomplish here is to provide an impression that will leave a lingering desire in your mind—a taste that will make you hunger for more.

Our mindset needs to be one of complete trust in His love. Trusting Him is the foundation for our faith.

My prayer is that God will reveal His salvation to you from faith to faith.[6] Faith to depend on His empowering work—and faith to know He watches over His Word to perform it.

Without faith it is impossible to please God. We must come to Him believing that He is everything He claims to be. It's critical that we expect His power to accomplish His will, no matter how impossible it appears to our human understanding. We must be fully persuaded of the creative power of God's Word and accept His testimony of who we are "in Christ." Our mindset needs to be one of complete trust in His love. Trusting Him is the foundation for our faith.

God must be the object of our faith, and we must believe that He has our eternal benefit in mind. We should acknowledge that He has the perfect plan for our lives and that He stands at attention to reward us when we **earnestly** and diligently seek Him.[7]

Let Your mercy *and* loving-kindness, O Lord,
be upon us in proportion to our waiting and hoping for You
(Psalm 33:22, AMP).

Are we like the psalmist, waiting in eager expectation for God to perform His purposes in our lives? Have we gone to His Word to gain understanding of the blessings we can expect? If we ignore His plan and refuse to accept our new identity in Christ, our ignorance will rob us of our trust in God and the faith inspired by that trust. As a result, we won't sit at our Lord's feet and eagerly learn from Him. We'll continue to allow our circumstances to speak louder than His Word.

If our faith is little, we will expect little. We won't invest an earnest effort in seeking God, and we'll have no expectation for Him to deliver as promised. Why would He reward someone who has such a trifling interest in receiving His promised gifts?

On the other hand, if we trust the intent of His heart and believe He has a perfect plan for our lives, we'll seek Him with great enthusiasm. Our attention will be focused on His Word, and the Word will become alive in us. We'll cry out for direction, and He will answer saying, "This is the way, walk in it."[8]

"For I know the plans I have for you," declares the Lord,
"plans to prosper you and not to harm you, plans to give you hope and a future.
Then you will call upon me and come and pray to me, and I will listen to you.
You will seek me and find me when you seek me with all your heart.
I will be found by you . . . and will bring you back from captivity"
(Jeremiah 29:11–14, NIV).

A loving Creator burns with passion over you. God has a brilliant plan for abundant life. The passion of His heart is to include you. He longs to open your eyes to deliver you from the darkness of mistaken identity.

A loving Savior yearns to cut you free from the cords that bind you—free from the seductive control of Satan.[9] The heavenly King of kings desires to grant you forgiveness for all your sins. He wants to purge your record of sin and forget about the past. He is watching you and waiting for you to ask.

If our faith is little, we will expect little.

A loving Father in heaven has prepared good gifts for you to enjoy here and now and an inheritance of incredible value for your future.[10] He wants to train you up in His ways, to empower you to conduct yourself in a becoming manner when you receive this inheritance.[11]

God wants you to be trained by practice—practice of His Word.[12]

Boot camp for eternity

Right here and now, Christians are living in a training camp. In some ways, we can compare our experience with a military boot camp where new recruits receive training in government authority, military discipline, and weapon usage.

The term *boot camp* stemmed from the required wearing of military-issued boots. New soldiers, drilled to exhaustion in this footgear, often find it difficult to appreciate the systematic training. The limits of human endurance are tested. The development of inner strength is demanded. Some soldiers question the value of boot camp experience. That is, until they enter battle. I recently saw a U.S. military pilot interviewed on television. An Iraqi missile had downed his plane, and the enemy had taken him captive. On camera, he credited his survival and eventual release to the training practices he endured in boot camp.

Life on earth is spiritual "boot camp" for the people of God. In the practice of His Word, we're trained for the battles of life and a much more critical mission—eternity. Our training ensures success on earth and our maturity to manage the eternal inheritance with wisdom. God promises that when He creates a new heaven and new earth, He will not permit sin to rise again.[13]

Only those trained by practicing His Word will understand the wisdom and love of God's eternal plan.

Only those trained by practicing His Word will understand the wisdom and love of God's eternal plan. The value of our training will be forever acclaimed. The heirs of eternal life will have learned through experience not to repeat the rebellion and sin that brought such horrible consequences. Only those trained by practice in His ways will be suited for God's eternal inheritance.[14]

In this analogy to boot camp, God's recruits are issued footgear. Our feet have been fitted with the gospel of peace.[15] We've been registered in the "Good News Camp." We're being trained in the authority of God's government and the disciplines of love, joy, peace, and obedience. The Lord of Hosts issues us weapons of spiritual warfare. These powerful weapons can take our thoughts captive and make them obedient to His will. Our weapons can pull down the vain arguments by which the enemy tries to build a stronghold in our minds.[16]

In our camp, it would seem some strategies of our Commander-in-Chief are difficult to understand. As members of the Lord's army, we think we should use all of *our* might in the battle. This error causes discouragement and exhaustion among our ranks. We miss the greatest aid of our training. In fact, we miss our most powerful weapon from God's arsenal. The secret weapon of God's plan is this: **He will do for us what we cannot do for ourselves.**

Unlike the U.S. military, God does *not* train His troops to draw on an inner reserve of human willpower. Rather, the Lord instructs us not to attempt anything in our own strength. He says that apart from Him, we can do nothing.[17] God wants us to depend totally on His power to overcome all the obstacles of our course. His power is made perfect in our weakness.[18] Our training prepares us to stand firm in faith, knowing the battle belongs to the Lord and that He will give us the victory.[19]

Drawing on God's strength is the only way to overcome our weakness—the only route to success in our training for eternity. The Bible says we're foolish to think we can perfect our walk by the power of our own flesh. Instead we must rely on the provision of the power of the Holy Spirit.[20] This is our most important strategy to avoid the enemy's missiles. Even if a surprise attack strikes and the enemy takes us captive, our only hope of survival and eventual release is to draw on God's power.

> *Our training prepares us to stand firm in faith, knowing the battle belongs to the Lord and that He will give us the victory.*

There's a second camp here on earth. It's a slave camp that some mistakenly call Camp Feel Good. Because this camp follows the downward trend of the world system, recruits find it easier to march in step with the majority and do what comes naturally. There's no rigorous training in discipline. Instead, people in this camp follow their own consciences and decide for themselves what's right and wrong. Since God's complete authority is not considered, they think they're walking in freedom from His laws—free to do as they choose.

They don't recognize that the master deceiver, Satan himself, is manipulating and controlling their actions. This evil leader prowls around plotting their destruction, while parading as an "angel of light."[21] He leads by deception, counterfeiting the good things of God[22] and promising freedom to his troops. Expecting freedom, these poor souls don't realize they've become slaves to corruption, "for a man is a slave to whatever has mastered him."[23] The deception is so cunning, the draftees of Camp Feel Good aren't aware they're walking in darkness along the broad path to destruction.

> *Salvation is a gift. There's nothing I can do to save myself. I'm saved by grace, through faith.*

"There is a way *that seems* right to a man, but its end is the way of death."[24] If they would only stop their march of madness and stand at attention to God, He would open their eyes and deliver them from the darkness of mistaken identity. God would bring them into His marvelous light and guide their steps to the narrow path of life.[25]

> "This is the covenant that I will make with them after those days, says the Lord: I will put My laws into their hearts, and in their minds I will write them," then He adds, "Their sins and their lawless deeds I will remember no more"
> *(Hebrews 10:16, 17, NKJV).*

Before God ever laid the foundations of the world, He knew how humans would exercise their gift of free choice. God had the "Calvary Plan" in mind before He created man.[26] He knew we couldn't save ourselves, so He opened a new and living way by which we could boldly return to His presence.[27] That way is the sacrificial blood of His only Son—the price He paid to buy you and me out of bondage. He did for us what we couldn't do for ourselves.

Salvation is a gift. There's nothing I can do to save myself. I'm saved by grace,[28] through faith in the completed work of Jesus Christ on the cross and His continuing intercessory work as High Priest.[29] That being true, the Bible still reveals eternal salvation is mine only if I obey God. "He became the author of eternal salvation to all who obey Him."[30]

> "Do we then by [this] faith make the Law of no effect, overthrow it or make it a dead letter? Certainly not! On the contrary, we confirm and establish and uphold the Law"
> *(Romans 3:31, AMP).*

How can God place conditions of obedience upon the promise of the gift of salvation? Why does He put His laws in my heart and write them on my mind? Jesus said if I break the commandments and teach others to do the same, I'll be called least in the kingdom of heaven.[31] In the New Testament book of James, I'm warned that if I break even one of His Ten Commandments, I'm guilty of them all.[32] Does a holy and righteous God ask more of me than I can deliver? The answer is revealed in God's perfect law of liberty.

The law of liberty—total dependence upon God

"But he who looks into the perfect law of liberty and continues in it, and is not a forgetful hearer but a doer of the work, this one will be blessed in what he does" (James 1:25, NKJV). The same author who wrote "break one . . . guilty of all" here tells me the secret of walking in God's will. I give glory to God for increasing my understanding about His perfect law of liberty. It's my compass and sets my heart free to walk in joy and without fear. God revealed that everything He expects of me, He has already empowered me to do.

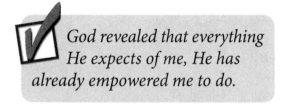

God revealed that everything He expects of me, He has already empowered me to do.

The law of liberty is this: I must recognize my absolute, total dependence upon Jesus Christ to perform a work in me that empowers me to walk in the commandments of God.

Listen to the advice of the apostle Paul:

> **Work out** [cultivate, carry out to the goal, and fully complete] **your own salvation with reverence and awe and trembling** [self-distrust, with serious caution, tenderness of conscience, watchfulness against temptation, timidly shrinking from whatever might offend God and discredit the name of Christ]
>
> *(Philippians 2:12, AMP).*

I used to read these words and cringe, because I didn't understand the law of liberty. Taking this advice out of context, I barely noticed the power of God's plan that Paul revealed with his continuing comments:

> [Not in your own strength] **for it is God Who is all the while effectually at work in you** [energizing and creating in you the power and desire], **both to will and to work for His good pleasure and satisfaction and delight**
> *(Philippians 2:13, AMP).*

Do you see the beauty of God's promise to us here? It is God who works in us to cause us to desire His will. As we draw near to Him, seeking instruction, He puts our will in perfect alignment with His. He changes the desires of our hearts. The Bible tells us we cannot change ourselves any more than a leopard can change its spots.[33] It's only by the power of the Holy Spirit that we can put to death the misdeeds of our flesh.[34] By God's grace and power, He will renew our minds and transform our attitudes and desires. And the promise goes much further—if we'll just cooperate with Him. Once our minds have been restored to His way of thinking, it's up to us to step out in faith. God will not force us to act. But if we'll take that first step, God promises His continued power to live in the way that pleases Him.

When I come to the Lord, asking Him to teach me His will, He works in me to line up my will with His.

Let me paraphrase this amazing promise of God found in Philippians 2:12, 13. When I come to the Lord, asking Him to teach me His will, He works in me to line up my will with His. The first phase of His powerful act is to renew my mind and place His desires in my heart. Then, I must work out the "saving grace" He has put in my heart, by one simple step. There's a "one-step" gap between my mind being renewed and walking in obedience to His will.

I must turn my willingness into resolve to take action—not depending on my own ability, but depending on the leading of His Holy Spirit. As I step out in faith, the second phase begins, and God pours out power from on high. By the power of His Spirit, I press forward and carry out the goals God has given to me to obtain His promises.[35] I walk according to His good pleasure, knowing that after I have done the will of God, He will make certain I receive the promise.[36]

Grace—our hope of glory

Our Lord said, "My grace is sufficient for you, for my power is made perfect in weakness."[37] He never expected us to walk the narrow road of salvation by our own power. Apart from Christ, we can do nothing to save ourselves. We can't obey God by our own power. Obedience is by grace. Grace is the unearned, undeserved gift of God. Grace is God's divine assistance—His supernatural power at work within us.

The two greatest gifts of grace that God has bestowed on us are Christ in us—our hope of glory[38]—and the power of His indwelling Spirit.[39] His grace is sufficient. He pours His life-giving power into us and perfects the good work He has begun in us.

> I know whom I have believed and am persuaded that He is able
> to keep what I have committed to Him until that Day
> *(2 Timothy 1:12, NKJV).*

We can walk in the law of liberty being confident of this very thing, "that He who has begun a good work in you will complete it until the day of Jesus Christ."[40] Praise God, salvation is all about Him and not up to us. All He asks of us is permission to work in us. Daily, we must choose to give Him permission by surrendering control of our lives to Him and walking in cooperation with His Spirit.

This wonderful law of liberty will keep us walking in obedience. We'll recognize God's commandments as His law of love—ten wonderful promises of what He will empower us to do. The joy of our salvation will be restored as we learn to depend totally on His power to work within us. With minds steadfastly fixed on God, we'll walk in perfect peace.[41] He frees us from condemnation.

> There is therefore now no condemnation to those who are in Christ Jesus,
> who do not walk according to the flesh, but according to the Spirit
> *(Romans 8:1, NKJV).*

The joy of our salvation will be restored as we learn to depend totally on His power to work within us.

Oh, how I pray that God is working in you—even now—what He also is working in me, through the understanding of His plan. The perfect law of freedom keeps me looking into the Word of God to learn who I am in Christ Jesus. By faith, I accept what God has to say about me.

By grace, I am who God says I am. Even if I don't see the evidence yet, I will do as He does—I will call things that are not yet tangible to my senses **as though they**

already existed.[42] Empowered by grace—and through my faith in Him—I put His Word into practice, and I'm blessed according to His promise. "But he who looks into the perfect law of liberty and continues in it, and is not a forgetful hearer but a doer of the work, this one will be blessed in what he does."[43]

The power of promise—
God watches over His Word to perform it

"I am the way and the truth and the life."[44] Jesus promises a way out of our identity crisis. In Him is life, and that life is the light of all men. Christ, the living Word, is the only way out of darkness. God sent His Word to heal us and deliver us from our destructive behavior.[45] The Word of God is life to us, bringing truth that has the power to change. As His Word enters our hearts, it sheds His light of understanding into the confusion of our darkness and shows us the way out.

As His Word enters our hearts, it sheds His light of understanding into the confusion of our darkness and shows us the way out.

Putting His Word into practice brings great blessings to our existing life and trains us for our eternal inheritance.[46] We've been promised the mind of Christ.[47] The Bible is the mind of Christ. The more we hide His Word in our hearts, the more we'll operate by the power of His mind.

Why would we want to lean on our own understanding, which is so pitifully inadequate? We have His great wisdom available to us. We must learn to lean on the authority and power of God's eternal Word.

"I make known the end from the beginning, from ancient times,
what is still to come. I say: My purpose will stand,
and I will do all that I please "
(Isaiah 46:10, NIV).

Then said the Lord to me,
You have seen well, for I am alert and active,
watching over My word to perform it
(Jeremiah 1:12, AMP).

> God watches over His Word to perform it. He will not let His plan be defeated.

God's overall purposes will stand firm. God watches over His Word to perform it. He will not let His plan be defeated. In fact, the Bible tells us that He regards everything He has planned to do as already being accomplished—even though the results have yet to be revealed to the physical senses of humanity.

God offers us new life through Christ—a glorious life now and forever. Still, He has made us agents of free will, and the Lord will not force us to accept His gifts. Instead, we must give Him permission to work in our lives. God intervenes by invitation. Invite Him in. He will work all things according to the wisdom of His plan.[48]

How do we know God's will, His plan for our lives? We can know the end from the beginning, because it is written in the Bible.

For this is the will of God, your sanctification
(1 Thessalonians 4:3, NKJV).

God's will for us is that we be separated from worldly evil, be sons and daughters who partake of His divine nature, and be holy. Can we achieve this? No way. Can He achieve this in us? Yes. If we'll only let Him have His way with us, He will do an incredible work in our lives. God's plan is to conform us to the very nature of His Son. Through the life of Jesus Christ, He plans to restore and establish humanity to the creation He originally intended.

When we receive Christ as our Savior, we have a spiritual union with Him.[49] God includes us—or positions us spiritually—in Christ.[50] Every single promise of God belongs to us if we're abiding "in Christ."[51] God works out all of the circumstances of our life for our **eternal** benefit, to help conform us to the image of Christ.[52] Our destiny is to become like Jesus. We must look to His Word—His promises—and see the vision of our new identity in Christ. To partake of His divine nature, we must grab hold of His promises and make them ours.

His divine power has given to us all things that pertain to life and godliness,
through the knowledge of Him who called us by glory and virtue,
by which have been given to us exceedingly great and precious promises,
that **through these** you may be partakers of the divine nature,
having escaped the corruption that is in the world through lust
(2 Peter 1:3, 4, NKJV).

Let's unpack all the promise of these two Scriptures. God has already equipped us with everything we need to do His will. His Spirit and His Word supply the divine power. Because of His loving character and righteousness, God has vowed to do for us that which we cannot do for ourselves.

The creative power of God is in His Word. God's promises empower us to escape evil. More precious than that, His promises bring new life in us and cause us to absorb the divine nature of Jesus Christ.

Hallelujah!

> *God has already equipped us with everything we need to do His will. His Spirit and His Word supply the divine power.*

The pathway to blessing

Know the truth, and the truth shall set you free. Amen?

Not so fast.

But, you think, *wait a minute . . . that's Scripture.*

Yes, it's Scripture taken out of context. Jesus said *if* we would **abide** in His Word, **then** we would be His disciples (disciplined followers) and **then** we would know the truth, and the truth would set us free.[53]

A simple acquaintance with His Word does us little good. The blessing comes from the knowledge we gain through living in His truths—the "knowing" gained through experiencing God in our daily lives.

> For you have need of endurance,
> so that **after you have done** the will of God,
> you may receive the promise
> (Hebrews 10:36, NKJV).

God's love is unconditional, but His promises are not. They're based on obedience to His will, which is the only pathway to blessing. What does the Bible say? **After** we've done the will of God, we'll receive the promise. That's why it's important to abide, or live in, God's truths.

Are we willing to conduct our lives for His glory? Will we choose to walk according to His instruction? If we do, we'll escape evil. If our practice is to live in

His Word, we'll partake of an ever-increasing measure of His divine nature. The Holy Spirit will lead us from one level of God's glory to the next.[54]

I get so excited about this glorious truth, I want to shout it from the rooftops! Just pause to consider it. All we have to do to overcome evil is to depend on God's power to live in His Word. He has vowed to give us the divine nature of Christ as we live in His promises. It's not us performing His Word—it is God fulfilling His Word in us by the power of His Holy Spirit. How much simpler could He have made His plan for our lives?

> God's love is unconditional, but His promises are not. They're based on obedience to His will, which is the only pathway to blessing.

We can stop grieving God. We can quit quenching and resisting His Spirit. We can be emptied of our old sin nature a little more each day, as we're trained for our glorious eternal inheritance. By simply choosing to obey, we can tap into a greater supply of the Holy Spirit. The more we obey, the more God gives us the supply of the Holy Spirit, and the more we become like Jesus.

And we are His witnesses to these things,
and so also is the Holy Spirit whom God has given to those who obey Him
(Acts 5:32, NKJV).

My heart breaks when I talk to Christians who feel defeated, discouraged, and unworthy. It doesn't have to be that way, if they only knew their identity in Christ. So few of us walk in the abundant life He wants to give us now, because we don't understand the privilege of obedience. Our all-loving, all-powerful Father God wants to do so much more than we have ever imagined. He is willing to do all things in us, for us, and through us.

It's critical we know who we are "in Christ." There's only one way to accomplish this. We learn our identity in Him by living in God's promises. This comes by experiencing a relationship of absolute dependence on God and His Word.

God wants His slumbering church, the members of Christ's body, to wake up and walk in true union with the living Word. It's time to abide in His Word, plant His promises, and allow God to bring His Word to life in us. God will reward those who earnestly seek Him in faith.[55] The promises of God are ushered into existence by faith.

Jesus said . . . "Did I not say to you that if you would believe you would see the glory of God?" *(John 11:40, NKJV).*

> *God wants His slumbering church, the members of Christ's body, to wake up and walk in true union with the living Word.*

Are you ready to live in absolute dependence upon the transforming power of His Spirit and His Word? The seed of the miracle is in God's Word.

Miracles from God will follow our faith when we overcome our identity crisis. God will be able to trust us with His power, just as He did with Moses and Joshua and Peter.

References

1. Exodus 14:22–31.
2. Joshua 10:12, 13.
3. Acts 5:15.
4. Hebrews 13:8; Malachi 3:6.
5. 1 Corinthians 6:17, NKJV.
6. Romans 1:17.
7. Hebrews 11:6.
8. Isaiah 30:21, NKJV.
9. Psalm 129:4.
10. James 1:17; Ephesians 1:18.
11. Acts 26:18.
12. Hebrews 5:14.
13. Nahum 1:9; Revelation 21:4, 27.
14. Revelation 14:12.
15. Ephesians 6:15.
16. 2 Corinthians 10:4, 5.
17. John 15:5.
18. 2 Corinthians 12:9.
19. Ephesians 6:13; 1 Samuel 17:47; 1 Corinthians 15:57.
20. Galatians 3:3.
21. 1 Peter 5:8; 2 Corinthians 11:14.
22. Matthew 24:24.
23. 2 Peter 2:19, NIV.
24. Proverbs 14:12, NKJV.
25. 1 Peter 2:9; Matthew 7:13.
26. Revelation 13:8.
27. Hebrews 10:20.
28. Ephesians 2: 8, 9.
29. Hebrews 7:20–28.
30. Hebrews 5:9, NKJV.
31. Matthew 5:19.
32. James 2:10–12.
33. Jeremiah 13:23.
34. Romans 8:13.
35. Philippians 3:12–14.
36. Hebrews 10:36.
37. 2 Corinthians 12:9, NIV.
38. Colossians 1:27.
39. Ephesians 3:16.
40. Philippians 1:6, NKJV.
41. Isaiah 26:3.
42. Romans 4:17.
43. James 1:25, NKJV.
44. John 14:6.
45. Psalm 107:20.
46. Hebrews 5:14.
47. 1 Corinthians 2:16.
48. Ephesians 1:11.
49. 1 Corinthians 6:17.
50. 1 Corinthians 1:30.
51. 2 Corinthians 1:20.
52. Romans 8:28, 29.
53. John 8:31, 32.
54. 2 Corinthians 3:18.
55. Hebrews 11:6.

Chapter 6
Planting God's Promises

You may have heard the story of an Eskimo and his two dogs. Different evangelists have told it, including Billy Graham, but I don't know where it originated. I'd like to share my version with you—I call it "Sinbad and the Junkyard Dogs."

Sinbad was a hard-hearted sort of fellow and a notorious gambler. He owned a junkyard and two prize-fighting dogs—a pit bull and a solid white German shepherd. Every weekend Sinbad took his animals out to the dogfights in the country. There he would match them against each other. Sinbad established the odds, and spectators usually placed their bets with him for the favored dog.

Often, the pit bull soundly whipped the German shepherd. However, sometimes the German shepherd pinned down the other dog within moments, rendering him helpless. Grady, a regular gambler, tried to pick the winner based on the odds. Poor Grady rarely won, and observed that Sinbad seldom had to pay off on the bets he accepted.

Fascinated and greedy for gain, Grady approached Sinbad and offered to purchase both dogs—on one condition. "I'll pay a handsome fee to buy them," he said, "if you'll just tell me your system for winning. I don't understand why the pit bull appears so much stronger on some weekends, but the shepherd beats the daylight out of him on others."

Once they agreed on the selling price, Sinbad grinned and said, "My system is easy. I simply feed one dog during the week and starve the other. The one who gets fed wins!"

 Our apathy grieves God.

The moral of this story applies to you and me. Do you recognize it? It might be helpful to review a similar message from the Bible: "For he who sows to his flesh will of the flesh reap corruption, but he who sows to the Spirit will of the Spirit reap everlasting life."[1]

We Christians have two natures within us: the old fleshly nature of sin and the born-again nature of Christ. If we feast on the trash of the world system, our sin nature rears its ugly head with the tenacity of a ferocious pit bull. In contrast, if we feed our new nature with the Word of God, the good Shepherd comes forth and wins the battle for us. The nature we feed wins.

The righteousness drought

Our holy and righteous Father abhors evil. He hates it because it's in direct opposition to His divine nature of love. God's heart is broken by the pain and suffering evil causes. Do you think His heart might also be torn by our attitudes toward evil?

"The fear of the Lord is to hate evil."[2] We have a problem. It seems Christians have lost reverent respect and awe of the Lord. We don't hate sin as God does. The vast corruption of our world has numbed our senses. In many cases, our response has been diluted to lukewarm indifference, shrugging shoulders, and clucking tongues. Our apathy grieves God.

It's difficult to avoid worldly images and influences. Are we vigilant to turn our eyes away from worthless things?[3] It breaks the heart of God when we allow earthly trash to gain entrance to our minds and pollute them.

Have we forgotten the Bible's warning that friendship with the world's system is hatred toward God?[4] One of Satan's subtle devices is to make sin humorous or entertaining. If he can put a cloak of comedy on sin and cause us to respond with laughter, the devil has scored. Our laughter demonstrates our approval of practices that go against God's righteous decrees.[5] Are we the devil's fool? Satan does all within his power to make sin appealing, wrapping it in a shiny foil package with a big satin bow. Do we have to open the package to realize that **sin is nothing more than gift-wrapped garbage?**

Oh, may God help us to hate evil as He does! Let us pray that we learn to discern between the pure and the impure. May He teach us His way of hating the sin, yet loving the sinner with a redemptive love. Let us pray ever more earnestly that we don't develop judgmental attitudes toward others.

None of us is righteous by our own merit.[6] We should all be saying, "There, but for the grace of God, go I." Judging others is nothing short of self-exaltation—the devil's favorite "trip wire" to cause our downfall. It's a sinister spirit of pride, the spirit of antichrist,[7] which is in direct conflict to the absolute humility of Christ. We should always be mindful of the counsel we've been given:

Let this mind be in you which was also in Christ Jesus . . .
He humbled Himself and became obedient to the point of death,
even the death of the cross
(Philippians 2:5, 8, NKJV).

Our enemy comes in like a flood, trying to knock us off our sure foundation. Pride is his greatest scheme to separate us from the Lord. Do we feed on the devil's fodder ourselves, while condemning others for *their* sins? How easy it is to fall into this trap. We must deprive our selfish, prideful nature, and partake of God's divine nature.

> He has given us His very great and precious **promises,**
> so that **through them** you may **participate in the divine nature**
> and escape the corruption in the world caused by evil desires
> *(2 Peter 1:4, NIV).*

By God's gracious and loving design, He has given us everything we need to live godly lives. He has a system for escaping evil, and He wants us to learn it. In drawing near to God, hiding His Word in our hearts, and living in His promises, we can escape the clutches of evil.

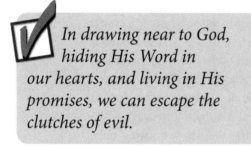

In drawing near to God, hiding His Word in our hearts, and living in His promises, we can escape the clutches of evil.

God seeks our cooperation. He wants us to depend on His power to develop the nature of Christ within us. His solemn vows are upon us—our destiny is to become like Jesus.[8]

Taking part in His divine nature requires our effort. It takes a vigorous, Spirit-empowered effort to plant God's promises in our hearts. We must sow to the Spirit to reap everlasting life. The Word of God is our nutrition for spiritual growth.

The potential of the harvest

We reap what we sow. We can't plant one thing and harvest something else. This law of God can't be violated in either the natural or the spiritual realm. Any farmer will tell you that if you sow wheat, you reap wheat. If you sow corn, you reap corn. Why? Because, **the potential of the harvest is wrapped inside the seed.**

> Do not be deceived, God is not mocked;
> for whatever a man sows, that he will also reap.
> For he who sows to his flesh will of the flesh reap corruption,
> but he who sows to the Spirit will of the Spirit reap everlasting life.

> And let us not grow weary while doing good,
> for in due season we shall reap if we do not lose heart
> *(Galatians 6:7–9, NKJV).*

Jesus told a parable about sowing seed (see Luke 8:4–15). It still has a very practical application to our lives today. As Christ explained the meaning of the parable to His disciples, He said, **"The seed is the word of God."**

Let me paraphrase the rest of His explanation. Some hear a message from God's Word and because the heart is burdened or hardened, the devil comes and easily snatches away the seed of the Word. Others hear a promise from the Bible and receive it with joy, but they don't cling to it long enough for it to take root. They lose faith as conditions challenge their belief. Sadly, they reject the eternal power and truth of God's testimony, and accept the conflicting evidence of their circumstances.

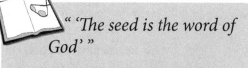 *" 'The seed is the word of God' "* *(Luke 8:11).*

Then there are those who sow His promises and, with their eyes on Jesus, the roots of faith are nurtured for a while. Yet, they allow their focus to be interrupted by the demanding hustle and bustle of life. Soon worldly matters creep in like weeds. Growing out of control, they overcome the mind. These "weeds and thorns" choke the life of God's Word out of their hearts. They quit trusting in His knowledge and return to their limited human understanding. Their growth as Christians is stunted, because they no longer acknowledge God's way of bringing them to maturity.

> Trust in the LORD with all your heart, And lean not on your own understanding;
> In all your ways acknowledge Him, And He shall direct your paths
> *(Proverbs 3:5, 6, NKJV).*

Any time we quit tending to the fertile ground of the kingdom of God within us,[9] we'll find we have sacrificed the good seed, His Word.

God designed the potential of the harvest to be wrapped inside the seed. You should pause to consider that: **All of your potential is wrapped inside God's Word.**

Sow the seed of God, His holy Word, into your heart. If you'll abide in His promises, He will make certain that the life-giving potential of His seed takes root and matures, developing the nature of Christ in you.

Therefore lay aside all filthiness and overflow of wickedness,
and receive with meekness the implanted word, which is able to save your souls.
But be doers of the word, and not hearers only, deceiving yourselves.
For if anyone is a hearer of the word and not a doer,
he is like a man observing his natural face in a mirror;
for he observes himself, goes away,
and immediately forgets what kind of man he was
(James 1:21–24, NKJV).

As Jesus concluded the parable of the sower and the seed, He said, "But the seed on **good soil** stands for those with a noble and good heart, who **hear** the Word, **retain** it, and by **persevering** produce a crop."[10] In this summary, Christ identifies for us the four steps necessary to plant His promises and partake of His divine nature:

1. Our hearts must be good soil, prepared for the planting.
2. We need a broadcasting system for hearing His Word and spreading His seed in our hearts.
3. We must receive and retain His promises.
4. We must persevere in His promises to produce the fruit of His Spirit—His divine nature—in us.

> *The seed of the miracle that changes us into the image of Christ is wrapped inside His Word.*

Let's take a closer look at these four critical steps for planting His promises. This is one of those great "systems of truth" God designed for us to overcome our identity crisis. The seed of the miracle that changes us into the image of Christ is wrapped inside His Word. The triumphant entry of His Word into our hearts will cause this miracle to start functioning.

Preparing good soil for planting

Most Christians believe they are "good soil" simply because they are the people of God. Yet, listen to what God said to His people of Judah and Jerusalem in the Old Testament:

> "Break up your fallow ground, And do not sow among thorns.
> Circumcise yourselves to the LORD,
> And take away the foreskins of your hearts"
> *(Jeremiah 4:3, 4, NKJV).*

Christianity has changed since the early church. We Christians are different—comfortable, complacent, compromising. It's easy to identify today's church age with the Laodicean church of Revelation, chapter three.[11] So many of us think we have it all and are in need of nothing. Uncircumcised hearts, lukewarm with indifference, keep us from understanding our identity in Christ and God's true purpose for establishing His church on earth.

This hardened attitude has left us with untilled ground. We're sowing among thorns—focusing our attention on the temporary things of this world, rather than on the eternal matters of God.

We can learn a lesson by looking at the ground of the earth. Exposed to the elements for a time without rain, the soil becomes hardened. In this condition, it's unfit for planting seed until it's plowed. We're not any different. When our focus shifts from depending on His Spirit and His Word, a spiritual dryness and certain hardening of the heart occur.

I can tell you from experience, when I've opened my heart to be exposed to the world's elements, I've quenched the living water of His Spirit.[12] The result was suffocating to spiritual growth. My heart became dry and crusty to the Word of God.

Jesus wants our hearts to be good soil—gardens committed to Him, plowed and ready for planting. Most of us have some area of our lives that needs plowing. The center of our heart may be "good soil," ready to receive His Word, while outside corners remain hardened.

For example, some may abide by His teaching on financial matters, but abandon the instruction to take our thoughts captive and guard our mouths. Others might accept all He has to say about salvation by grace, but deny the requirement of obedience to His commandments. Then there are those who walk in obedience to His law, but reject the love and forgiveness He wants to pour into our hearts for others.

God is love,[13] and God is holy. His Spirit is the Spirit of love and holiness. We must recognize any action that is not motivated by love and holiness is not of God.

> **A loving Creator desires that we put forth an earnest effort to seek Him and know the good plan He has for our lives.**

Because we sow among thorns, we spoil God's harvest of righteousness in us. And the heart of our heavenly Father is breaking. "I thought you would call me 'Father' and not turn away from following me."[14]

God wants to cut away the thorns of worldly habits and attitudes. He wants our hearts to be plowed and pliable, so we can receive His seed—His Word. A loving Creator desires that we put forth an earnest effort to seek Him and know the good plan He has for our lives. If we're willing, He is ready and able to conform us to the image of His Son, Jesus Christ. The heart of our Father longs to send showers of blessings upon us. He waits for our cooperation.

> Break up your fallow ground, For it is time to seek the LORD,
> Till He comes and rains righteousness on you
> *(Hosea 10:12, NKJV).*

Only plowed ground is fit for planting seed. We need to put our hand to the plow. Here are some steps I've found helpful in turning over, or tilling, my heart for God:

1. Experience the joy of repentance. With all of life's demands, it's easy to let priorities get out of order. Some people are surprised when I tell them that I wrestle with this problem, even though I work in full-time ministry. As with any profession, I can allow my work efforts to take top priority and find I've sacrificed the intimacy of my relationship with Christ. The awareness of the presence of my constant Companion is missing.

Whenever I've forsaken Jesus Christ as my "First Love," I become painfully aware of how far I've fallen. In the past when this occurred, I allowed the devil's arrows of guilt and condemnation to penetrate my heart, and shame kept me at a distance from God. Now that I understand the perfect "law of liberty," I have learned the joy of repentance. I come before God, humbly confessing my sin and acknowledging my total dependence upon His power. He gives me a new beginning and wipes my record clean. Praise God—"His compassions never fail. They are new every morning."[15]

2. Pray to be filled with His Spirit. I ask God to forgive me for grieving or resisting His Holy Spirit—or, if need be, to forgive me for quenching His Spirit.[16] I ask Him to cause me to die to self and live for Him. I pray that by the power of His Holy Spirit, I will put to death the misdeeds of my flesh[17] and be emptied of self. Then I pray that the Holy Spirit will give me an understanding of God's spiritual words and teach me His will. I ask to know His character and His plan, and to be taught who I am "in Christ." I ask the Lord to fill me with His Spirit. Jesus said,

> "Ask and keep on asking and it shall be given you;
> . . . how much more will your heavenly Father give the Holy Spirit
> to those who ask and continue to ask Him!"[18]

3. Pray to be sanctified by His Word. When Jesus prayed to the Father for us, He said, "Sanctify them by Your truth. Your word is truth."[19] As I pick up the Word of God, I always try to remember this prayer and make it mine. I ask God to do a sanctifying work in me through His Word, creating a pure and undivided heart in me. I pray God will give me power to overcome, and I give Him permission to *cause* me to be all that He has *called* me to be.

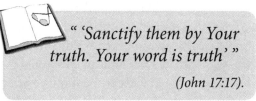

" 'Sanctify them by Your truth. Your word is truth' "

(John 17:17).

4. Pray for the desire to read the Bible. I ask God to give me an unquenchable desire for His Word—a prayer He is eager to answer. I acknowledge His Word is life to me, asking Him to open my spiritual eyes and give me His wisdom.

As I humble my heart before the Lord in this manner, He makes it good soft soil. He teaches me to trust Him and lean on His understanding. The Spirit and the Word are ready to come with a demonstration of His power to change me.

Broadcasting the seed of His Word

When the soil is ready, it's time for the seed. God will not disappoint us when we approach Him with a plowed heart. He will expand our trust in Him and give us an increased measure of faith in His testimony. That faith comes as we meditate on His Word. When the Bible says, "Faith comes by hearing," it doesn't mean that hearing produces faith. Hearing is better compared to the hand that broadcasts the seed.

Have you ever used your hand to broadcast flower or vegetable seeds in a garden? I've seen many folks sow wildflower seeds by casting them in this way, and it fascinates me to see the patches of flora come up in season. My gardening skills aren't the best, so I choose seedlings to plant. I figure, since they've already sprouted, they have a better chance of surviving my care. Yet I do recall an exciting experience I had in witnessing some dried-up seeds burst forth with life.

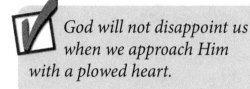

God will not disappoint us when we approach Him with a plowed heart.

When I was in the third grade, I was curious where the seeds for pinto beans came from. My teacher explained the beans we ate were actually the seeds for the beanstalk. She also said that if we planted these beans in sun-warmed soil and kept them moist, they would sprout back to life. My nine-year-old mind had a difficult time grasping how those dead looking beans could produce a live plant. I wanted to see for myself, so I set up an experiment.

Taking several pinto beans, I wrapped them securely inside a cotton dishtowel, set them on the windowsill in the sunlight, and moistened them daily. In a few weeks, I peeked inside the towel and found they had germinated. To my delight, there were little green sprouts coming out of each bean.

The experiment wasn't performed because I had great faith those pinto beans would sprout. Rather I had faith in my teacher, who appeared to be smarter than I was. Her words had seemed impossible of fulfillment, but her explanation made me seek an experience with the truth. Faith was ushered in by hearing that the possibility existed—and by trusting in the person who told me. Through that small window of faith, I witnessed what seemed like a miracle to me—dried-up old beans were transformed into living plants.

I've heard people refer to the Bible as a "bunch of dead letters." Remarkably, even notable figures within the evangelical community have echoed that sentiment lately. These confused souls promote the idea of worshiping "in spirit and in truth"[20] as a concept that is above the Word of God and one that requires little attention to the "old writings" of the Bible. Such comments are blasphemous. I pray the Lord will open the eyes of His professed followers to the life-giving power of His Word. Obedience to God's Word is the highest possible expression of worship for God.

Jesus said,

"The Spirit gives life; the flesh counts for nothing.
The words I have spoken to you are spirit and they are life"
(John 6:63, NIV).

God says there is life in His Word. If we want to worship in spirit and in truth, we need to worship in the Word—making the Bible our primary focus. Jesus is the Word become flesh. He calls the Word "spirit," and He calls the Word "life." It is by the power of His Word that we are sanctified by His truth and develop His holy nature. The counsel of God's Word is eternal. Bible writings are **not** inoperative words of the past.

For the word of God is living and powerful, and sharper than any two-edged sword, piercing even to the division of soul and spirit, and of joints and marrow, and is a discerner of the thoughts and intents of the heart
(Hebrews 4:12, NKJV).

My pinto beans appeared lifeless to a mind that could not comprehend the miracle of life stored within them. Likewise, the Word of God appears lifeless to those without comprehension—to those without the Spirit of God. The Bible is God's message to His creation. The writings are inspired spiritual words, understood only by the help of the Holy Spirit.[21]

I don't want to sound harsh with my comments about those who call the Bible "dead letters." I'm not judging the motivation of these poor souls. Rather, by the Word of God, I can determine their actions are wrong.

Jesus would reply to these individuals saying, "You are in error because you do not know the Scriptures or the power of God."[22] Christ warned us:

Be careful what you are hearing.
The measure [of thought and study] you give [to the truth you hear]
will be the measure [of virtue and knowledge] that comes back to you—and more
[besides] will be given to you who hear
(Mark 4:24, AMP).

We must be careful what we hear. We should always measure the message by the Scriptures. It doesn't matter how much theological training a person has, there can be no understanding without the Spirit of God. We must guard our hearts to prevent scholarly credentials from swaying us.

There is only one standard for truth—the Holy Bible.

> Consequently, faith comes from hearing the message,
> and the message is heard through the word of Christ
> *(Romans 10:17, NIV).*

The broadcast system God uses to spread seeds of faith is "hearing" His Word. Hearing introduces the message of God's love and His wonderful plan for our lives.

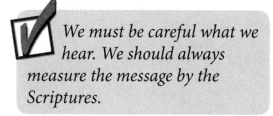

We must be careful what we hear. We should always measure the message by the Scriptures.

But as we've already seen, hearing alone does not produce faith. When the seed of His Word is broadcast, it will not take root and develop faith unless our soil is good.

Do you want more faith? Open your heart to God's broadcasting system and invest more time in hearing. Church sermons, Bible studies, Christian television, radio programs, tapes, and books. These are all wonderful tools to renew the attitudes of our minds.

The most effective broadcasting system I've discovered is the hearing of my own voice. I generally read the Bible aloud as I study. This practice increases my focus and causes my ears to open and receive God's Word.

When I discover a promise of God, I lay hold of it and claim it for myself. Then I return God's Word to Him as an affirmation. This affirmation is a declaration, confirming that I accept what God has to say about me as absolute truth. For example, when I read 2 Corinthians 5:17, I might say, "Thank You, Father, for including me in Christ. Thank You, Lord, for making all things new. I am a new creation in Christ. My old nature has passed away, and my new nature has come."

Hearing my own voice speaking God's Word is the greatest way, I've learned, to usher in faith. We will examine the benefits of this more closely in chapters seven and eight.

For now, the most critical point to recognize is that we should approach God in absolute trust when we come to the Scriptures. Our challenge is to learn **not** to lean on our own understanding. We need to abandon human opinions and ask God to give us His wisdom, by the power of the Holy Spirit.

Much of what God says seems impossible of fulfillment from our limited human viewpoint. Our minds should readily accept God's Word, believing in His testimony as being from Almighty God, who cannot lie.

> *Much of what God says seems impossible of fulfillment from our limited human viewpoint.*

Receiving and retaining His promises

Let's review where we are in the process of planting God's promises. To plow up the hardened areas of our heart, we've come before the Lord in humility and repentance, acknowledging our dependence upon His Spirit. Next, we've allowed God to broadcast the seed of His Word into the soil of our hearts through hearing His Word. Now we're ready to move on to a third, critical step.

We have to **receive** God's Word as a promise of what He will accomplish, and we have to **retain** it—grab hold of it and not let go. This is the action step that releases His creative power into our life. Let me illustrate what I mean by recounting an historical event.

One of the most amazing acts of faith recorded in the Bible is that of a young Jewish girl who had the trust to receive an incredibly personal word from God. When an angel appeared and told this virgin she would give birth to God's Son, she was troubled and curious as to how it would happen. The angel explained that the Holy Spirit would overshadow her and concluded,

> For with God nothing is ever impossible and
> no word from God shall be without power or impossible of fulfillment
> *(Luke 1:37, AMP).*

The original Greek text of this verse reads: "No word from God is void of power." Listen to this young girl's response: "I am the Lord's servant," Mary answered. "May it be to me as you have said."[23] What incredible trust in God and belief in the power of His Word. Notice what the Bible records about the amazing faith Mary demonstrated when she received and retained His Word:

> " 'I am the Lord's servant,' Mary answered. 'May it be to me as you have said' "
>
> *(Luke 1:38. NIV).*

Blessed is she who has believed that what the Lord has said to her will be accomplished! *(Luke 1:45, NIV).*

Scripture often refers to God's Word as "seed" (lower-case "s") and to Christ as the "Seed" (upper-case "S") of God.[24] When Mary received the Word of God, His Seed was planted in her. She held fast to His Word. Then the power of the Holy Spirit overshadowed her and the purpose of God's Word was birthed in her. She brought forth the Son of God. "The Word became flesh."[25]

What if Mary had merely believed that all things are possible with God, but had thought, *Surely He can't mean that it will happen to me!* What if she had disregarded God's Word—rejecting His "Seed" and His purpose for her life? There's no doubt that God would have found another handmaiden to fulfill His plan, but Mary's history would have to be rewritten.

God's Word has creative power—life-changing power. Still, that power cannot be released in you unless you're willing to receive and retain the seed He has for you.

It's a dangerous thing to reject God's testimony about who we are in Christ. We need to remember that the Bible warns that if we don't accept God's testimony, we're regarding Him as a liar.[26] Come to Him believing that He exists and has the power to do all that He vows to do. He rewards those who earnestly seek Him with this attitude.[27]

If we receive the Word "seed" of God and pray for the Holy Spirit to overshadow us with the power of God, the Creator will cause us to become pregnant with expectancy. He wants to birth the purposes of His Word in us. He wants His Word to become flesh in our lives.

Persevering to produce a harvest

Finally, what causes God's promises to take root in our hearts and produce a harvest of righteousness? Perseverance!—determined by the *level* of belief we have.

There are different degrees of belief. One is mere mental assent. In other words, it's arriving at that point where we accept something as true, but having no personal experience with it. A greater degree of belief is when we receive truth and apply it personally. I can better explain this by sharing a story I once heard when I was young.

A famous circus star was renowned for his tightrope acrobatics and performed for heads of state and large audiences throughout the world. To make his act even more daring, he always performed without a net. During one evening performance, he pedaled a bicycle across a high wire with a young woman sitting on the handlebars.

"Spectacular," the crowds cheered, "Bravo!" Suddenly, the star climbed down from the high wire and approached the crowd. Going to a heavyset man on the front row, he explained what he proposed to do for his next act. He intended to walk across the same wire, pushing a three hundred pound man in a wheelbarrow. "Do you believe I can accomplish this?" he asked the star-struck admirer.

> *Believing in Jesus for salvation means to "be living in" Jesus.*

"Absolutely," the man answered with confidence. "Good," said the circus star, "then hop in!"

Obviously, hopping into the wheelbarrow would require a greater degree of belief. Do you see the point this illustrates? When you reach the greater level of **"believing in"** a truth, you are willing to **"be living in"** that truth. Our most vital necessity as Christians is to apply this greater level of belief to God's Word.

The Bible testifies, "For God so loved the world that He gave His only begotten Son, that whoever believes in Him should not perish but have everlasting life."[28] This wonderful promise is referring to a belief that is much greater than mental assent. It requires a degree of belief that receives His Word as truth and personally applies it. You have to be willing to hop into the wheelbarrow.

Believing in Jesus for salvation means to "be living in" Jesus. Do you want proof?

> You believe that there is one God. Good!
> Even the demons believe that—and shudder.
> You foolish man, do you want evidence
> **that faith without deeds is useless?**
> *(James 2:19, 20. NIV).*

It's not enough simply to agree that Jesus is the Son of God and died to pay the penalty for our sin. To receive God's gift of salvation, we must *receive* Christ as our personal Savior and make it our practice to *be living in* Him.

The same principle applies to His Word. It's not enough to agree that the Bible is the Word of God. We must *receive* His Word, planting His promises in our heart.

Then we must hop into the wheelbarrow and *be living in* His Word, applying His Word through daily practice.

"Little children, let no one deceive you. He who practices righteousness is righteous, just as He is righteous."[29] We deceive ourselves if we think just knowing *about* God and knowing *about* His Word will save us. We're made righteous by faith in Christ. His righteousness working in us will cause us to *practice* righteousness—to act in His right way of doing all things.

God's love is unconditional, but His promises carry a condition of obedience to His will.

> For you have need of endurance, so that **after** you have done
> the will of God, you may receive the promise
> *(Hebrews 10:36, NKJV).*

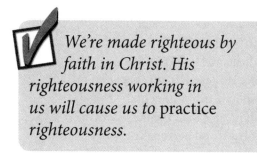

We're made righteous by faith in Christ. His righteousness working in us will cause us to practice *righteousness.*

We don't have to worry if we will just cooperate with Him. A loving God will empower us to do all He has asked us to do. As we plow up our hearts and expose them to His love, God will cause us to seek the Word. When we sow to the Spirit, God will empower us to receive and retain His seed. As we step out in faith-actions, the Holy Spirit will empower us to put God's Word into practice. As we persevere, God will do a creative act of renewal in our hearts.

> This is what the kingdom of God is like. A man scatters seed on the ground.
> Night and day, whether he sleeps or gets up, the seed sprouts and grows,
> though he does not know how. All by itself the soil produces grain—
> first the stalk, then the head, then the full kernel in the head
> *(Mark 4:26–28, NIV).*

God gives the increase in the growth.[30] It is God who will finish the good work He has begun in us[31] and establish His harvest of righteousness in our lives. Doesn't that make you want to shout with joy?

God nurtures our development by the living water of His Spirit.[32] Then as we persevere in His promises, He causes the miracle-working function of the Word to reproduce Christ's nature in us. By His power, we are kept as a well-watered garden—the fruitful vineyard of the Lord.

> In that day sing . . .
> "A vineyard of red wine!
> I, the LORD, keep it, I water it every moment;
> Lest any hurt it, I keep it night and day"
> (Isaiah 27:2, 3, NKJV).

> *As we persevere in His promises, He causes the miracle-working function of the Word to reproduce Christ's nature in us.*

Christ Jesus (the Seed of God) is reproduced in our hearts through His Word (the seed of God) and the living water of the Holy Spirit.

The process amazes me. I plant a promise in my heart and put His Word into practice. Then one day a little seedling stalk suddenly springs forth. His Word is alive and active in me, causing me to be living in His truth. I've witnessed that God works this way in all who plant His promises and persevere. His life continues to grow and mature in us. We're led from one level of sharing in His divine nature to the next. Hallelujah!

Harvest hope

God's purposes are unchanging. There is certainty in His promises. This provides us hope—an eager expectation—that God will perform His Word in us, even though we have yet to see the evidence. The Word, alive and active in us, is our hope of developing His character and fulfilling our destiny.

> Because God wanted to make the
> unchanging nature of his purpose very clear to the heirs
> of what was promised, he confirmed it with an oath.
> God did this so that, by two unchangeable things
> in which it is impossible for God to lie,
> we who have fled to take hold of the hope
> offered to us may be greatly encouraged.
> We have this hope as an anchor for the soul, firm and secure.
> It enters the inner sanctuary behind the curtain, where

> Jesus, who went before us, has entered on our behalf.
> He has become a high priest forever. . . .
> Therefore He is able to save completely
> those who come to God through Him,
> because He always lives to intercede for them
> *(Hebrews 6:17–20; 7:25, NIV).*

Hope in God's promises is the anchor for our souls, keeping us from being double-minded. Christ, the Living Word, is able to save us completely. He will sustain our growth by the rich power of His Word[33] and His Spirit.

Remember:
- You can reap only what you sow.
- The potential of the harvest is wrapped inside the seed.
- All of your potential is wrapped inside God's Word.
- God will produce a harvest of righteousness in you.

Isn't it time to start planting His promises?

References

1. Galatians 6:8, NKJV.
2. Proverbs 8:13, NKJV.
3. Psalm 119:37.
4. James 4:4.
5. Romans 1:32.
6. Isaiah 64:6.
7. Isaiah 14:13.
8. Romans 8:29.
9. Luke 17:21.
10. Luke 8:15, NIV.
11. Revelation 3:14–22.
12. John 7:38.
13. 1 John 4:16.
14. Jeremiah 3:19, NIV.
15. Lamentations 3:22, 23, NIV.
16. Ephesians 4:30; Acts 7:51;
    1 Thessalonians 5:19.
17. Romans 8:13.
18. Luke 11:9, 13, AMP.
19. John 17:17, NKJV.
20. John 4:24.
21. 1 Corinthians 2:13, 14.
22. Matthew 22:29, NIV.
23. Luke 1:38, NIV.
24. Galatians 3:16.
25. John 1:14.
26. 1 John 5:10.
27. Hebrews 11:6.
28. John 3:16, NKJV.
29. 1 John 3:7, NKJV.
30. 1 Corinthians 3:7.
31. Philippians 1:6.
32. John 7:38, 39.
33. Hebrews 1:3.

Chapter Seven
Rhema Affirmations

There is one thing for certain: Miracles followed the authority of the words of Christ. Nicodemus recognized this. He believed the young carpenter was a teacher from God and possibly Someone far greater. Yet, as a ruler of the Jewish council, Nicodemus wasn't ready to make a public confession of faith. He waited and approached Jesus secretly, to tap in to the apparent wisdom of God. Even the cover of night couldn't hide his startled expression when Jesus spoke these words:

> I tell you the truth, no one can see the kingdom of God unless he is born again. . . .
> I tell you the truth, no one can enter the kingdom of God unless he is born of water
> and the Spirit. Flesh gives birth to flesh, but the Spirit gives birth to spirit
> *(John 3:3, 5, 6, NIV).*

What a shocking statement—words beyond the capacity of human understanding! Nicodemus thought it was irrational and questioned the truth of it. Christ spoke in spiritual words. To the natural mind, they seemed to be abstract foolishness. The Bible explains that the unspiritual man cannot receive the divine thoughts of God. Only those who have been born-again—who have the Holy Spirit dwelling within them, teaching and explaining His spiritual words—can discern God's thoughts.[1]

There's a notable exception to this principle. Every human can understand and welcome the plan of salvation **before** they've been born again of the Spirit. God designed the evidence of His creative power, and His love and amazing grace, to penetrate the natural heart and mind. The Holy Spirit is constantly at work to bring conviction of sin.[2] He strives to lead all of humanity to the turning point of godly sorrow and to draw them near to God.[3]

The kindness of God offers the gift of repentance to those dead in their sins.[4] But beyond the evidence of a Creator and the understanding of His plan of redemption, the sacred truths of the Bible can't be known without the indwelling of the Holy Spirit. To see divine wisdom, we must focus the Spirit's spiritual lens of understanding on the Bible.

What did Christ mean by His words to Nicodemus? Sometimes we overlook a familiar passage of Scripture, thinking we know it. There's a divine depth to the thoughts expressed in the Bible, and we should be cautious of taking a casual approach to our studies. I pray often that God will give me an unquenchable desire for His inexhaustible Word. I want to go deeper into His mind, gaining a more intimate relationship with His thoughts.

 "Seeing" a kingdom truth is the first stage.

Some years ago, I found myself drawn to our subject text. I asked the Spirit of God to increase my understanding. Now, I want to share a ray of light the Spirit shone on this passage to expose truth I hadn't recognized before.

Christ defined the two stages required for receiving the truths of the kingdom: Seeing and entering. We must be born again by the Spirit of God to see kingdom truths. We have to *see* before we know how to *enter*.

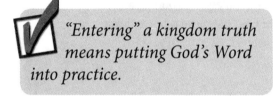 *"Entering" a kingdom truth means putting God's Word into practice.*

"Seeing" a kingdom truth is the first stage. By the insight of the Holy Spirit, we can understand God's Word. But seeing is not enough. What good does it do to recognize the blessing of humility, if we remain prideful? What is the benefit of knowing God's counsel for a healthy lifestyle, if we ignore it? Seeing the truth is just a platform, or a springboard, for us to go to the next stage.

"Entering" a kingdom truth means putting God's Word into practice. It requires a step of faith. Empowered by His Spirit, we enter His truth as we do the will of God. This same standard of action was discussed in chapter six. Planting His promises in good soil and persevering for the harvest is *entering* His truths. Hopping into the wheelbarrow is the identical principle. If we're "believing" in His Word, we must "be living in" His Word. That's what it means to have entered the kingdom truths of God.

A profound, yet simple teaching

Speaking Scripture as affirmations is a practice the Holy Spirit inspired me to begin in 1995 when I was so desperately ill. After tapping into the inherent power of this exercise, it has become my passion. God has trained my focus on His Word, replaced my thoughts with His thoughts, and expanded my vision of His plan. I "see" the kingdom of God. An increased understanding has prompted me to step out in faith and *enter* God's kingdom truths.

The practical application of this teaching is so simple. All we have to do is accept God's testimony about us as new creations in Christ Jesus. Then as we find a promise of God in the Bible, we simply speak His Word over our lives.

I would like to note that all of His commandments are promises also. For example, God's command—"in your anger do not sin"—is also a promise of what God will empower us to do. We can turn this commandment into an affirmation, and say

> Thank You, Father, that I am not controlled by anger.
> Thank You for the power not to sin. Sin is not my master.
> I am empowered by the grace of God
> *(Ephesians 4:26; Romans 6:14, paraphrased).*

Part of the beauty of these affirmations is that they change the way we think and talk about ourselves. When you behold—in the mirror of the Word—the reflection of who you are "in Christ" and declare it with your living voice, the amazing result is that you become what you behold!

> But we all, with unveiled face,
> beholding as in a mirror the glory of the Lord,
> are being transformed into the same image
> from glory to glory, just as by the Spirit of the Lord
> *(2 Corinthians 3:18, NKJV).*

Humans have a natural tendency to focus on the negative. If you doubt that, let me ask you a question. If the phone rings in the wee hours of the morning, say around 2:30 A.M., do you expect it to be good news? When that happens, most of us are seized by a sense of alarm and expect a bad report, isn't that true? And, when something negative does happen in our lives, we often rehearse it in our minds until it consumes our thoughts and life energy.

Jesus said, "Therefore do not worry about tomorrow, for tomorrow will worry about its own things."[5] That's a commandment, which is also a promise of what Christ will empower us to do. The apostle Paul puts it this way:

> Do not be anxious about anything, but in everything,
> by prayer and petition, with thanksgiving, present your requests to God.
> And the peace of God, which transcends all understanding,
> will guard your hearts and your minds in Christ Jesus
> *(Philippians 4:6, 7, NIV).*

When we learn to speak God's Word over our lives, we learn to lean on His understanding, and He directs our paths.[6] Practicing these affirmations of God's promises will change your life. God guarantees it!

> *When we learn to speak God's Word over our lives, we learn to lean on His understanding, and He directs our paths.*

If it's so simple, you might wonder why I'm going into such depth in this chapter and the next to explain the process. That's a good question. Why should you invest your time in this study? Why do you need to know the depths of truth that support a simple effective process?

I've learned that we won't continue practicing any process unless we understand why and how it benefits us. I receive reports from many Christians who've been empowered by turning Scripture into affirmations. Yet this exercise of walking in the Word is a challenge to continue, and they abandon it and slip back into old lazy habits. Some time later, in response to God's leading, they start up again. That's when I hear from them. Excited Christians contact me and say, "I don't understand why I ever quit practicing this. It's so powerful and makes such a difference in my life."

I understand what they're saying. My experience has been the same. Until I appreciated why this practice exerted such a powerful force, I wasn't compelled to continue. When the Spirit helped me to see this as my way to "plug in" to the power of God, it became worth the effort. I devoted the time and energy to enter this kingdom truth. To encourage my effort, the Lord impressed this thought upon me: **Time is life. How you invest your time is how you invest your life.**

How are you investing your life? The affirmation process is worth the investment of your time. It will work the very mind of Christ in you.[7] Jesus said that His words are "spirit and they are life." The transforming power of God's Word will change your life forever. You'll be clothed with power from on high.[8]

I pray the Holy Spirit will help me communicate the underlying power of this process and its many benefits in a way that you can grasp for His glory. I've condensed a lot of deep thought into this single chapter. Because it's somewhat technical, I'll warn you in advance that it's not an easy read. But please don't give up on me.

> *When the Spirit helped me to see this as my way to "plug in" to the power of God, it became worth the effort.*

We will be laying a foundation in this chapter that will help you understand chapter eight—"Benefits of Rhema"—a chapter I promise you'll enjoy. In fact, I think of the next chapter as the crowning jewel of this entire study. For now, what I ask of you is your patience. I pray as we go to the bottom of this teaching, the Spirit will stir the anointing in you and teach you concerning all things.[9]

> God has revealed them to us through His Spirit.
> For the Spirit searches all things, yes, the deep things of God
> *(1 Corinthians 2:10, NKJV).*

I'm not writing this chapter for you to store the depth of the teaching in your memory. It's being written for only one purpose: That you may be convinced of the power of the process, so that you can abide in His Word through *rhema* affirmations. (You'll learn a bit later just what *rhema* is all about.)

Would you like to come with me and dive deeper into the divine reasoning of God?

English translations

I have a friend who speaks both the English and Spanish languages fluently. Hearing a song she sang in Spanish, I asked her to translate the verse into English. "It doesn't translate," she said. I'm not sure I fully understand her reply. But, one thing I do recognize is that in some ways the English language is limited, in comparison to other languages of the world.

For example, the Greek language can be far richer than English in some respects. Our single English word *love* covers a number of different Greek words that provide nuances of meaning. In Greek, there's a word for unconditional love, a different word for brotherly love, another word for the affectionate love of a friend—and the list goes on. When the New Testament was translated from Greek, we lost some of the rich undertones of these multiple words that are translated into English simply as "love."

I'm not a Greek scholar. In fact, I've never had formal training in the study of the Greek language. But I am a student of the Bible. My love for the Word of God has motivated me to purchase many study guides—commentaries, lexicons, and dictionaries—written by various Greek scholars.

I study the Bible using several different translations at the same time. To see which English translation provides the fullest expression of meaning, I compare the verses to the original Greek text. When I began this method of study, in the fall of 1999, what I learned caused me to self-publish *Life Affirmations from Scripture.* That book included nearly two hundred affirmations (a sampling of which is included in the appendix to this book). I felt compelled to share the affirmations immediately. I had been speaking them for several years and recognized the inherent power in the practice but remained in the dark as to why their impact was so dramatic—until I studied the underlying Greek of these verses.

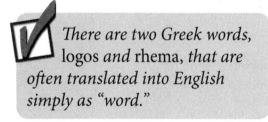

There are two Greek words, logos *and* rhema, *that are often translated into English simply as "word."*

What I uncovered is of great interest. There are two Greek words, *logos* and *rhema,* that are often translated into English simply as "word." Was it possible, I wondered, that a deeper study of these two Greek words would increase my understanding? As I began to dive into the study, I found a pearl of great value.

Rhema affirmations defined

It wasn't the scholarly definition of these Greek words—*logos* and *rhema*—that fascinated me most. Instead, it was the way Scripture applied these words. As I reviewed every New Testament reference containing the English word *word,* and then checked the underlying Greek word, I began to see a fine distinction between the use of *logos* and *rhema.*

I believe the Holy Spirit inspired the choice of words penned by Bible writers. There are subtle nuances in the application of these two Greek words. What I discovered helped me understand why affirming God's Word brings renewed vitality and power to my Christian experience.

Let me explain how I constructed the following definitions. In part, they were derived from multiple sources, including *Vine's Expository Dictionary of Old and New Testament Words, Strong's Concordance, Word Meanings in the New Testament,* and *Word Pictures in the New Testament.* An equally important component of my attempt to define these terms came from their distinctive application within Scripture.

- **Logos** *(Greek, pronounced "log'-os")—translated—***Word** *(English).*

    The word *logos* implies the **sum** of God's revelation to humanity. It's the vast unfolding of the reasoning and power of the mind of God. *Logos* is the expression of His will and His purposes. The entire content of the Bible is the "logos" Word of God, also referred to as the "Word of life" in Philippians 2:16. Jesus is also called the *Logos* ("Word") of God. In Christ, we find the perfected revelation of God to humanity.

    > *The term* logos *implies the* **sum** *of God's revelation to humanity.*

- **Rhema** *(Greek, pronounced "ray'-mah")—translated—***Word** *(English).*

    The word *rhema* implies a single item—a **specific** word spoken by God with an applied purpose, a word of God that has a practical and immediate function. A personal word of instruction from God is a "rhema" Word. For example, when Jesus told Simon to launch into the deep and cast out his fishing nets, he replied, "Master, we have toiled all night and caught nothing; nevertheless at Your word *[rhema]* I will let down the net" (Luke 5:5, NKJV).

    > *The word* rhema *implies a single item—a specific word spoken by God with an applied purpose, a word of God that has a practical and immediate function.*

In the next chapter, an interesting pattern will develop that will make the difference between these two Greek words more evident. The use of these words within Scripture indicates that we can apply any instruction or promise of God—any verse of the entire Bible (the "logos" Word) intended for God's corporate body of believers—as a "rhema" Word.

Where we're concerned, we plant His "logos" Word in our hearts, and it springs to life as a practical "rhema" Word to us. Our *rhema* utterance brings out a single verse of the Bible, confessed by our living voice and personally applied to our lives.

> ☑ *Our* rhema *utterance brings out a single verse of the Bible, confessed by our living voice and personally applied to our lives.*

I need to add a caveat here—we cannot apply to ourselves a *specific* "rhema" Word meant only for a *specific* individual. For example, Mary received a "rhema" Word from God that she would give birth to the Messiah. We can't be so foolhardy as to think this can be applied to our lives today.

The distinction between these two Greek words will become much clearer as we continue. In the next chapter, "Benefits of Rhema," we'll examine them in the context of Scripture and let the Bible develop the definition for us. I believe you'll see the exciting advantages of taking God's "logos" Word and making it our *rhema* utterance. I've come to appreciate that this is the way His Word enters our lives with triumph and helps us achieve the overcoming victory.

There's also a difference between "claiming" God's promises and speaking His Word as a *rhema* affirmation. Claiming a promise of God is recognizing your right to it. By faith, we've been given a "title deed" interest in all of God's promises, if we're living in Christ. God wants us to recognize and stake our claim on what He has vowed to give us in His Son.

> Now faith is the assurance (the confirmation, the title deed)
> Of the things [we] hope for, being the proof of things
> [we] do not see and the conviction of their reality—
> faith perceiving as real fact what is not revealed to the senses.
> (*Hebrews 11:1, AMP*).

A *rhema* affirmation goes beyond claiming. It's a confession—a word of faith—that declares we agree with God's wisdom. As we confess His Word with our living voice, we confirm that it is our life source. It causes us to exalt God's Word over our human wisdom and opinion. Then He causes His way of thinking to become our way of thinking. As we plant and practice His promises, we validate God's testimony.

A *rhema* affirmation is a confession of who we are in Christ, a confirmation that says, "I am not who I think I am. I am not who you think I am. **I am who God says I am.**"

Rhema affirmations transform us by the renewing of our minds.[10] They help us to know and understand the perfect will of God. Hearing our living voice declare the wonders of His truths increases our faith. As we reprogram our thoughts in this way, His Word becomes our source for truth, and we overcome our identity crisis. The life-giving power of the Word washes away the influence of the world system.[11] The Word of God that we affirm becomes a fire that burns away the dross, separating the pure from the impure.[12]

> ✔ *A* rhema *affirmation goes beyond claiming. It's a confession—a word of faith—that declares we agree with God's wisdom.*

The ultimate blessing is that as we apply His promises personally, we partake of His divine nature. This all begins by the power of our tongue.

> The tongue has the power of life and death,
> and those who love it will eat its fruit
> *(Proverbs 18:21, NIV).*

We speak life into our days when we speak God's Word into every situation. On the other hand, just like the Israelites at the edge of the Promised Land, we speak death into our days if we endorse the devil's testimony of doubt and disbelief.

Do the words of our mouth really matter to the Lord? "Say to them, 'As I live,' says the LORD, 'just as you have spoken in My hearing, so I will do to you: The carcasses of you who have complained against Me shall fall in this wilderness.' "[13]

> "I say to you that for every idle word men may speak,
> they will give account of it in the day of judgment.
> For by your words you will be justified,
> and by your words you will be condemned"
> *(Matthew 12:36, 37, NKJV).*

Almost daily, I find myself confessing the sin of idle words—those that escape my lips and the "unspoken words" of my thoughts. Words that don't line up in agreement with His will. Words that are void of His power. I seek God's forgiveness and ask Him to put a guard at the door of my mouth.[14] I pray the Word of faith will be in my heart and on my tongue.

> "The word is near you; it is in your mouth and in your heart,"
> that is, the word of faith we are proclaiming
> *(Romans 10:8, NIV).*

I ask God to cause me to confess His testimony as my source of life through *rhema* affirmations. My constant prayer is that I will speak into all situations with the tongue of an instructed disciple.[15]

Creative word power

The prophet Jeremiah said, "God made the earth by His **power;** He founded the world by His **wisdom** and stretched out the heavens by His **understanding**. . . . Ah, Sovereign LORD, You have made the heavens and the earth by Your great power and outstretched arm. Nothing is too hard for You."[16]

What was the dynamic power by which God created the world?

> By God's word *[logos]* the heavens existed and the earth was formed
> *(2 Peter 3:5, NIV).*

> In the beginning was the Word *[logos]*, and the Word *[logos]* was with God,
> and the Word *[logos]* was God. All things were made through Him,
> and without Him nothing was made that was made.
> And the Word *[logos]* became flesh and dwelt among us
> *(John 1:1, 3, 14, NKJV).*

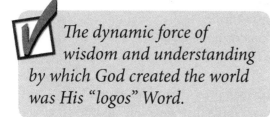

The dynamic force of wisdom and understanding by which God created the world was His "logos" Word.

The dynamic force of wisdom and understanding by which God created the world was His "logos" Word. The Bible testifies that the power responsible for the creation of all things was none other than Christ Jesus, the "Logos" Word of God. Christ spoke the reasoning and purposes of His mind and created something from nothing, an act that only God can do. He first spoke the "logos" Word to create the heavens and the earth. Yet,

> The earth was without form, and void; and darkness was on the face of the deep.And the Spirit of God was hovering over the face of the waters
> *(Genesis 1:2, NKJV).*

> By faith we understand that the worlds were framed by the word ["rhema" Word] of God
> *(Hebrews 11:3, NKJV).*

When it was time to equip and perfect His creation, the Lord became very specific with His commands. The dynamic energy of God's *rhema* commands—"Let there be"—caused the completion of creation, equipping and perfecting all things. The practical application of the "rhema" Word of God put the framework on His creation.

> *The dynamic energy of God's rhema commands— "Let there be"—caused the completion of creation, equipping and perfecting all things. The practical application of the "rhema" Word of God put the framework on His creation.*

Further still, the Bible tells us the mighty "rhema" Word of Christ sustains and upholds all things:

> He is the perfect imprint and very image of [God's] nature, upholding and maintaining and guiding and propelling the universe by His mighty word *[rhema]* of power
> *(Hebrews 1:3, AMP).*

God has a *rhema* command to the earth that keeps it in its orbit and another that is His law of gravity. He has a *rhema* command to the oceans that says, "You can come this far and no farther." God has a *rhema* command for every object of His creation. Everything is sustained by His mighty "rhema" Word power.

What about us? The Bible says that when we're born again, we are God's work of art, re-created in the image of Jesus Christ, to do the good works and walk in the path He planned in advance for us.[17] How does God re-create us? When we look to our own experience with the creative power of God's Word, we find an interesting parallel to the creation process of our world:

> Having been born again, not of corruptible seed but incorruptible,
> through the word *[logos]* of God which lives and abides forever
> *(1 Peter 1:23, NKJV).*

By His will, God chose to give us new birth through His "logos" Word of truth.[18] Our rebirth is generated when we receive and welcome the Word of God, implanted and rooted in our hearts.[19] We're not saved by our works of righteousness. Scripture says that by His mercy, we're saved through the washing of rebirth and renewal by the Holy Spirit.[20] When we were born again, God made something of nothing—taking us dead in sin and making us alive in the Spirit—making us a new creation in Christ Jesus.[21] At our rebirth we're just like little babies; we're not the finished product. We still require the daily process of continued change that conforms us to His image.

Just as the creation of the heavens and earth begged completion, we also need the perfecting work of the Lord. We're like a new lump of clay. We should entrust our lives to the master Potter's hands. Who are we to question the wisdom of the Creator's great design? "For shall the work say of him that made it, He made me not? Or shall the thing framed say of him that framed it, He had no understanding?"[22]

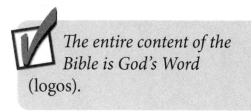

The entire content of the Bible is God's Word (logos).

The master Architect stands ready to equip us, to complete and perfect His work in us. The Creator of the universe stands ready to uphold and sustain us by His mighty "rhema" Word of power.

Let me summarize these conclusions about the creative power of God's Word from the study of these two Greek words:

- The **"logos"** Word of God created the earth from nothing.
- The **"rhema"** Word of God completed the work, establishing the framework and upholding it.
- The **"logos"** Word of God made us new creations in Christ.

- The **"rhema"** Word of God (that which we personally apply to our lives) equips us and perfects us, brings order into our lives and transforms us into His image.

> *Making His Word rhema means to focus on individual Bible promises, confess them over our lives, and put them into practice.*

The entire content of the Bible is God's "logos" Word. Jesus said the "logos" Word is truth meant for our sanctification, to separate us from sin and set us apart for God.[23] It's defined as alive and active, and sharper than a two-edged sword.[24] In the next chapter, we'll learn how to draw out this Word and use it as the sword of the Spirit. The "logos" Word in our hearts becomes our weapon for righteousness when we draw it out as *rhema* and personally apply its power.

Making His Word *rhema* means to focus on individual Bible promises, confess them over our lives, and put them into practice. In the next chapter, we'll develop a clearer understanding of the power of this process. For now, we should just recognize there's power in the "rhema" Word to equip us and complete the good work that God has begun in us.

We have ventured into some depth of this teaching. Now let's surface and take a deep breath. Here are the five main points I would like you to recall:

- By the grace of God, you are who God says you are. Accept His testimony as truth. Go ahead and say it right now: *I am who God says I am!*
- You can take His *logos* Scripture from the Bible and apply it as a *rhema* affirmation. This is taking the wisdom and counsel of God's testimony and personally applying it to your life.
- The power of life and death is in your tongue.
- If you confess His Word, God will confirm His Word. Your act of faith grants God permission to complete and perfect His creative work in you.
- His mighty "rhema" Word of power will sustain and uphold you.

As I said earlier, this is a profound—yet simple—teaching. Thank you for staying with me as I tried to escort you into the depth of His creative Word power. We've laid a foundation for understanding the rest of our study. It might be more appropriate to say we've set the table, because in the next chapter we're going to feast on the goodness of God's Word.

As you learn the dynamics of this process, I believe that you'll become like that precious ancient patriarch, Job. You'll esteem and treasure the Word of God more than your daily food.

Oh, yes, let me remind you—creative miracles do follow the authority of the Word of God!

References

1. 1 Corinthians 2:10–14.
2. John 16:8.
3. 2 Corinthians 7:10.
4. Romans 2:4.
5. Matthew 6:34, NKJV.
6. Proverbs 3:5, 6.
7. 1 Corinthians 2:16.
8. Luke 24:49.
9. 1 John 2:27.
10. Romans 12:2.
11. Ephesians 5:26.
12. Jeremiah 23:28, 29.
13. Numbers 14:28, 29, NKJV.
14. Psalm 141:3.
15. Isaiah 50:4.
16. Jeremiah 10:12; 32:17, NIV.
17. Ephesians 2:10.
18. James 1:18.
19. James 1:21.
20. Titus 3:5.
21. 2 Corinthians 5:17.
22. Isaiah 29:16, KJV.
23. John 17:17.
24. Hebrews 4:12.

Chapter Eight
The Benefits of *Rhema*

Have you ever taken a bite of food that is so delicious you want to share the experience with someone you love? If I've ordered a scrumptious treat at a restaurant, I instantly turn to my husband and say, "Ummm! Taste and see how good this is!" He doesn't always share my enthusiasm, and I'm disappointed when he refuses the offer. I usually follow up with, "Are you sure? You don't know what you're missing."

As a Christian, I'm excited to share the goodness of God that I've tasted. Like King David, I want to burst forth and say, "Oh, taste and see that the Lord is good; blessed is the man who trusts in Him!"[1] The Bible speaks of those "who have tasted the goodness of the word *[rhema]* of God and the powers of the coming age."[2]

I can't wait to share a sampling of the benefits of God's "rhema" Word. Here's a quick overview from the eight Scripture references we'll be reviewing:

- *Rhema* confession increases our faith.
- The "rhema" Word is our spiritual nutrition.
- The "rhema" Word sustains and upholds us.
- *Rhema* washes away the influence of the world.
- The "rhema" Word is the "sword of the Spirit."
- *Rhema* increases the effectiveness of prayer.
- No "rhema" Word is impossible of fulfillment.
- It's dangerous to reject the "rhema" Word.

I see the Bible, God's "logos" Word, as a smorgasbord of sacred nutrition laid out buffet-style for me. Here He has provided everything I need for life and godliness.[3] Yet, I'd die of starvation if I merely looked upon this divine dining arrangement. To gain spiritual strength, I have to fill my plate and partake of His promises for myself.

The "rhema" Word is those Scriptures that I take personally—confessing them and putting them into practice. That's what brings spiritual nutrition to me. That's how I taste and see the goodness of God's Word, and the powers of the coming age. And once I've tasted, I hunger for more.

> He has bestowed on us His precious and exceedingly great promises,
> so that **through them** you may escape (by flight) from the moral decay . . .
> that is in the world because of covetousness (lust and greed),
> and become sharers (partakers) of the divine nature
> *(2 Peter 1:4, AMP).*

Scripture says, "If you do not stand firm in your faith, you will not stand at all."[4] Great spiritual stamina will be required to endure the closing trials of this world. How can we stand firm in faith? Do you recall the story in chapter six about the pit bull and the German shepherd—the two fighting dogs? I used that as an analogy of the two natures within us, warring against each other. The moral of that story is simple: The nature we feed is the one left standing as the victor. Which nature are you feeding?

> For he who sows to his flesh will of the flesh reap corruption,
> but he who sows to the Spirit will of the Spirit reap everlasting life
> *(Galatians 6:8, NKJV).*

> He who sows sparingly will also reap sparingly,
> and he who sows bountifully will also reap bountifully
> *(2 Corinthians 9:6, NKJV).*

The Bible speaks of tasting the heavenly gift and becoming partakers of the Holy Spirit.[5] Oh, how I long to increase my share in God's gifts of grace! I want to be like Jesus. I choose to participate in His divine nature. I prefer to partake of a greater measure of the Spirit and His power. But I must first prepare room to welcome Him, by being emptied of self.

God can fill me with the Holy Spirit only to the degree that I've become void of my selfish, sinful nature. I can't put to death the misdeeds of my flesh by human effort alone. I need the help of an executioner. The Bible says

> For if you live according to the sinful nature, you will die;
> but if **by the Spirit** you put to death the misdeeds of the body, you will live
> *(Romans 8:13, NIV).*

As the Lord gives me the provision of His Spirit, it is by His power that I can put to death my old nature and make room for a greater infilling. I've learned that walking in obedience to God is the only way to snuff out the old nature and to be filled with the Holy Spirit. The Spirit of love and righteousness can have no fellowship with lawlessness.[6] This explains why Scripture says God gives the Spirit to those who obey Him.[7]

> *I've learned that walking in obedience to God is the only way to snuff out the old nature and to be filled with the Holy Spirit.*

I believe that, like me, you also hunger to partake of God's heavenly gifts. Like me, you desire to understand how Christ can perfect His power in your weakness.[8] We want His life to be reproduced in us, and we cry out for the solution to our dilemma. Our answer comes from looking to His Word as our life source.

> It is the Spirit who gives life; the flesh profits nothing.
> The words that I speak to you are spirit, and they are life
> *(John 6:63, NKJV).*

We can listen to sermons from now till "kingdom come," and we won't be partakers of His divine nature unless we ***plug in*** to God's power source—proclaiming His promises as our personal testimony and putting His life-giving Word into practice. Let me share an experience that will illustrate our need to do this.

Within the walls of my otherwise cheery kitchen, there was a dreary corner. Overhead lights only cast shadows on the area, and sunlight streaming from opened windows didn't reach there. It was depressing to me, so I purchased a brightly colored Tiffany lamp for the table in the corner.

This may sound silly, but plugging it in for the first time was a real joy. The whole kitchen appeared livelier and more beautiful. In fact, the lamp became the focal point of the room. It became my habit to leave the lamp on even during daylight hours—just because it was so cheery.

One day, I walked into my kitchen, and the lamp was dark. I quickly changed the light bulb—still no light. A thought was impressed upon my mind. *What do you see?* I could only see the leaded outlines of the design. There was no depth of color, and the artwork seemed lifeless. Leaning over to check the wall outlet, I discovered that the cord had been disconnected. As I plugged it in and stood up, another thought struck me. *Now what do you see?* Focusing again on the lamp, I saw a luminescent creation of beauty with vibrant colors. The multifaceted design had come to life.

You and I are like that lamp. God created us in His image. We are a marvelous and complicated design. Yet, unless we are "plugged in" to His power source, we are colorless, and the intent of God's design within us is lifeless. When we *plug in* to His power source, God's handiwork can be seen within us, and we shine with His radiance.

King David knew his source of light:

> For You, O Lord, are my lamp; the Lord lightens my darkness
> *(2 Samuel 22:29, AMP).*

> The entrance *and* unfolding of Your words gives light;
> it gives understanding—discernment and comprehension—to the simple
> *(Psalm 119:130, AMP).*

We need to "plug in" to our power source—His life-giving Word. *Rhema* affirmations are the most efficient connection. They transfer His mighty energy to us and convert us to His way of thinking.

We need to "plug in" to our power source—His life-giving Word. Rhema affirmations are the most efficient connection.

Personal application of God's Word has transforming power. There's one comment that I hear repeatedly after I've shared this teaching and others have practiced it: "Wow! This is powerful!"

Oh, I want you to taste and see how good the "rhema" Word of God really is! As we speak His Word in our living voice, He renews our minds. Worldly thoughts and attitudes are washed away. Whispers of our past are silenced. Our sense of identity "in Christ" is deepened.

As we speak His Word with our living voice, He connects our thoughts to His plan for our lives. We're filled by His power. We begin concentrating all of this energy on pressing forward to attain the goals of God's will.[9] By the power of His Word and His Spirit, we are transformed.

And do not be conformed to this world,
but be transformed by the renewing of your mind,
that you may prove what is that good
and acceptable and perfect will of God
(Romans 12:2, NKJV).

The practice of *rhema* affirmations requires discipline. But it's well worth the effort. There's a high return on the investment of your time. Remember that the Bible, in its entirety, is the "logos" Word of God. The Word becomes *rhema* for us when we focus on a verse, confess it with our living voice, and personally apply it to our lives.

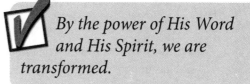

By the power of His Word and His Spirit, we are transformed.

Before you can enter this kingdom truth, you have to see it. You must be convinced it has merit based on Scripture. The Bible reveals that this practice can bring many wonderful benefits.

For your consideration, I've selected eight Bible passages that refer to the "rhema" Word of God. Come with me now, and let's review some of them.

1. ***Rhema* confession increases our faith.**
   - Romans 10:8–10, 17, NKJV:
   "But what does it say? 'The word [**"rhema" Word**] is near you, in your mouth and in your heart' (that is, the word [**"rhema" Word**] of faith which we preach): that if you confess with your mouth the Lord Jesus and believe in your heart that God has raised Him from the dead, you will be saved. For with the heart one believes unto righteousness, and **with the mouth confession is made unto salvation. . . .**

   So then faith comes by hearing, and hearing by the word [**"rhema" Word**] of God."

Let's unpack the promise of this Scripture. What's in our mouth? What's the "word of faith"? The "word of faith" refers to Scriptures of God that we confess with our living voice—the Word that has become *rhema* to us. With our mouths, we confess the testimony of God over our lives. Our confession is made unto salvation.

How does faith come? By hearing the "rhema" Word of God spoken.

If I tell you that your destiny is to become like Jesus, my words may not penetrate your heart. But if you take God's testimony from Romans 8:29 and by *rhema* affirmation say, "I am predestined by God to be conformed to the image of Jesus," this promise will grow and flourish in your heart. Our confession increases our faith. And the promises of God are ushered into existence by faith.

> *Our confession increases our faith. And the promises of God are ushered into existence by faith.*

Take 2 Corinthians 5:17 as another example. If you apply this verse personally and confess, "I am a new creation in Christ. The old has gone and the new has come," you might meet some mental resistance at first. We're painfully aware of our own shortcomings and failures. We don't always feel like the old has gone.

But remember: we can't trust our feelings! We must remember that God considers it done, because His power is being exerted to complete the good work He has begun in us.[10] He knows the end from the beginning and works all things according to His will.[11] Therefore, He regards things that have yet to be completed as if they were already done.[12]

And since we have the same spirit of faith, according to what is written,
"I believed and therefore I spoke," we also believe and therefore speak
(2 Corinthians 4:13, NKJV).

With the spirit of faith we also "call those things which do not exist as though they did," because God has revealed to us the purposes of His heart. When we know His plan and confess His testimony over our lives, God works a miracle in us.

The potential of the harvest is in the seed. All of your potential is wrapped within the seed of His Word. As we repeat His promises aloud, He begins to wipe away our old attitudes and thoughts, replacing them with His thoughts. The life of Christ begins to form in us.[13] His creative Word power gives us the wisdom of Christ and amazingly shapes His image within us.

Let the word of Christ dwell in you richly in all wisdom
(Colossians 3:16, NKJV).

In chapter six, when I referred to methods of broadcasting seeds of faith through hearing the Word, perhaps you noticed an obvious omission. Sermons and Bible studies were mentioned. Christian television, radio programs, tapes, and books were included. My top proposal was confessing His Word aloud. What's missing from this list? I purposely omitted memorizing Scripture.

Although memorization is an excellent way to plant the seeds of faith, I didn't consider it because so many people are put off by the suggestion of memorizing Scripture. Traveling from church to church, I've polled many congregations. Less than 1 percent of members say they enjoy memorizing Scripture. I felt I'd be whistling in the wind to suggest a method that intimidates most of us—including me.

> Meditate on these things; give yourself entirely to them,
> that your progress may be evident to all
> *(1 Timothy 4:15, NKJV).*

The Bible counsels us to meditate on His Word—considering what it means to us, what it reveals about the character of God and His plan, and reflecting upon who we are "in Christ." There's no commandment to memorize. Still, memorizing Scriptures is a wonderful process for those who will work through it. The majority of us won't. In fact, I think if we would quit referring to Scripture as a "memory text" and start referring to the Word as "life" to us, more people would wake up and take notice. We would begin to recognize the Scriptures as the solemn vows of God—what He desires to accomplish in our lives, and will accomplish, if we give Him permission and cooperate.

The potential of the harvest is in the seed. All of your potential is wrapped within the seed of His Word.

> But the word is very near you,
> in your mouth and in your heart, that you may do it
> *(Deuteronomy 30:14, NKJV).*

Affirming the Scriptures isn't a mechanical repetition of a text, and it's not mind over matter. It's coming to God's Word as our source of life-giving power and elevating His thoughts above our own reasoning. As we absorb the Word into our hearts and return it to Him with our living voice, He empowers us to do all that He requires of us. Then He bestows the blessings of abundant life.[14] He promises His Word will not return empty, because He is watching and waiting to perform it in those who have faith to accept His testimony.

> So shall My word be that goes forth from My mouth;
> It shall not return to Me void,
> But it shall accomplish what I please,
> And it shall prosper in the thing for which I sent it. . . .
> I am watching to see that my word is fulfilled
> *(Isaiah 55:11, NKJV; Jeremiah 1:12, NIV).*

The benefit of *rhema* affirmations is that we begin taking God's testimony personally. As the Word becomes our testimony, it becomes more relevant to us. We overcome by the blood of the Lamb and the Word of our testimony.[15]

People frequently ask how I've memorized so much Scripture. They want to know my system. Here's the answer. I never set out to memorize. Instead, I just speak His Word as *rhema* affirmations, and the results are amazing. The Word of God has become my source of life. It has become alive and rooted in my heart through this process.

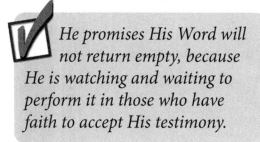

He promises His Word will not return empty, because He is watching and waiting to perform it in those who have faith to accept His testimony.

It can work in this manner for anyone. Recently an elderly man, challenged by lack of memory, began this practice. Within a couple of weeks, he exclaimed, "I'm remembering Scripture for the first time in my life, and all I set out to do was to speak it."

At the end of this book, I've included an excerpt from *Life Affirmations from Scripture*—the book I published in 1999 and that is now available in a new edition as a companion volume to the book you're reading. I encourage you to test this process for yourself. Set aside twenty to thirty minutes each day for a month and see what happens. I can promise you one thing—if you'll be consistent in this practice, you'll discover that the power of speaking the "rhema" Word of faith results in hiding God's Word in your heart. I also believe you'll be amazed at your increased measure of faith.

2. The "Rhema" Word is our spiritual nutrition.

- Matthew 4:4, NKJV.

"But He answered and said, 'It is written, 'Man shall not live by bread alone, but by every word [**"rhema" Word**] that proceeds from the mouth of God.' "

Our spiritual nutrition comes from entering in and practicing God's Word. We must take the "logos" Word personally and make it *rhema* to us. The vitality of our Christian life directly relates to the amount of His promises we digest—bringing them into our hearts and minds, and confessing them as the "rhema" Word of faith.

> ✓ *The vitality of our Christian life directly relates to the amount of His promises we digest.*

Jesus invites us to dine with Him. "Behold, I stand at the door and knock. If anyone hears My voice and opens the door, I will come in to him and dine with him, and he with Me."[16]

> Your words were found, and I ate them,
> And Your word was to me the joy and rejoicing of my heart;
> For I am called by Your name, O LORD God of hosts
> *(Jeremiah 15:16, NKJV).*

Largely, faith depends on knowledge of His Word. Faith expects very little when God's Word is unknown. Still, we must be mindful there are different dimensions of knowledge and belief. There's the "mental assent" dimension that sees and accepts the Bible as truth. The greater dimension is when we enter into His truths through personal application.

It's possible to be very religious and still be suffering from spiritual starvation. Earlier we considered the life of the Pharisees and saw this principle at work. They had the Scriptures memorized word for word. Yet, most were not divinely nourished because they didn't partake of the Word as their life sustenance. Likewise, I have a friend who has attained a doctorate in theology, the highest academic degree awarded in the study of the Bible. Yet, she has no personal relationship with the Lord and gains no spiritual nutrition from the Word.

> But you, son of man, hear what I say to you.
> Do not be rebellious like that rebellious house;
> open your mouth and eat what I give you
> *(Ezekiel 2:8, NKJV).*

As Christians, we're either strong or weak, depending on the amount of God's Word that is alive in us and that we practice daily. Our Lord said we "live by . . . every word ["rhema" Word] that proceeds from the mouth of God." When His Word becomes *rhema* to us, it brings down the veil that clouds our vision, the veil of guilt that keeps us from entering into His presence. In addition, something amazing begins to develop.

> But we all, with unveiled face,
> beholding as in a mirror the glory of the Lord,
> are being transformed into the same image from glory to glory,
> just as by the Spirit of the Lord
> *(2 Corinthians 3:18, NKJV).*

Through the nourishment of the Word, and by the power of the Spirit to practice it, we begin to mature in the image of Christ. Becoming involved in this process has caused me to gain a true appreciation for Job's declaration:

> I have not departed from the commandment of His lips;
> I have treasured the words of His mouth more than my necessary food
> *(Job 23:12, NKJV).*

3. The "Rhema" Word sustains and upholds us.
- Hebrews 1:3, AMP.

   "He is the sole expression of the glory of God—the Light-being, the out-raying of the divine]—and He is the perfect imprint and very image of [God's] nature, upholding and maintaining and guiding and propelling the universe by His mighty word ["rhema" Word] of power."

Before we focus on "His mighty word ["rhema" Word] of power," I just have to take a moment to comment on the first part of this Scripture. I love this verse. It opened my eyes to see my heavenly Father for who He really is.

I grew up without a father figure. My father, a pilot, died in a plane crash when I was six years old, and my stepfather was an abusive alcoholic. As a youth, I was taught I had to be perfect for my heavenly Father to love me. I thought He watched over me constantly, ready to punish me and cast me away from His presence. Although I loved and trusted Jesus, my thoughts toward God the Father were ones of fear and anxiety—until I discovered this Scripture.

How liberating it was to learn my Father God is exactly like my tender, loving Savior—holy and righteous, yet filled with love, mercy, compassion, and patience. I could write a book on this topic alone, but we'd better move forward on this teaching.

Our subject verse says that Christ sustains everything in the universe by His "rhema" Word of power. By personal experience, I can testify this is true. Every Scripture that has become *rhema* to me sustains and upholds my walk with the Lord and the quality of my life on earth. There are so many examples to choose from, I'm hard pressed to decide which Scripture to use. Let's look at one of my many favorites.

> *Every Scripture that has become* rhema *to me sustains and upholds my walk with the Lord and the quality of my life on earth.*

You will keep him in perfect peace,
whose mind is stayed on You, because he trusts in You
(Isaiah 26:3, NKJV).

I took this promise and made it a *rhema* affirmation by saying, "Thank You, Father, for keeping me in perfect peace. Thank You for keeping my mind steadfastly fixed on You. I do trust You, Lord. I know You have my eternal benefit in mind."

After I had confessed this over my life for a while, I had a situation pop up that robbed me of peace. I fretted and wrung my hands for about an hour. Then the Lord suddenly brought this Scripture to my remembrance. And this thought was impressed upon my mind by that still, small voice of the Holy Spirit:[17] *Where are your eyes focused—on Me or on the circumstances?*

I recognized why I had lost my peace, and I turned my eyes upon Jesus, the Author and Finisher of my faith.[18] My peace was restored instantly. His mighty "rhema" Word of power kept me in peace throughout a difficult trial.

Christ will not only sustain *you* by the mighty "rhema" Word of power, He will also give you the tongue of an instructed disciple and a word of His love that will support other weary souls.[19] My intimate relationship with His Word has empowered me to give godly counsel—instruction based on His wisdom, rather than human wisdom. God has taught me how to share His love, encouragement, and comfort with others. He has increased my wisdom through His "rhema" Word.

> *When we have real hope in the promises of God, we'll be anchored, and we won't be double-minded.*

There's no comparison between knowing God's Word as "head knowledge" and knowing His Word through experience as "heart knowledge." When the Scriptures become our "rhema" Word of faith, it causes our hearts to bubble over with hope. He is the God of hope.[20] Hope is the eager expectation that God will perform His Word.

Because God wanted to make the unchanging nature of His purpose
very clear to the heirs of what was promised, He confirmed it with an oath.
God did this so that, by two unchangeable things
in which it is impossible for God to lie,
we who have fled to take hold of the hope offered to us may be
greatly encouraged.
We have this hope as an anchor for the soul, firm and secure
(Hebrews 6:17–19, NIV).

What does an anchor do for a ship in a stormy sea? It helps it stay the course. When we have real hope in the promises of God, we'll be anchored, and we won't be double-minded. "If any of you lacks wisdom, let him ask of God, who gives to all liberally and without reproach, and it will be given to him. But let him ask in faith, with no doubting, for he who doubts is like a wave of the sea driven and tossed by the wind. For let not that man suppose that he will receive anything from the Lord; he is a double-minded man, unstable in all his ways."[21]

Let us hold fast the confession of our hope without wavering,
for He who promised is faithful
(Hebrews 10:23, NKJV).

When God's Word becomes *rhema* to us, the level of trust we have in His faithfulness soars. Our hearts will overflow with hope, and the power of Christ's "rhema" Word will sustain us in all situations.

> The Lord gives voice before His army . . .
> For strong is the One who executes His word
> *(Joel 2:11, NKJV).*

4. *Rhema* washes away the influence of the world.
  • Ephesians 5:25–27, NKJV.
  "Christ also loved the church and gave Himself for her, that He might sanctify and cleanse her with the washing of water by the word ["rhema" Word], that He might present her to Himself a glorious church, not having spot or wrinkle or any such thing, but that she should be holy and without blemish."

JD and I lived in Dallas for the first five years of our marriage. We frequently made the long trip to his family's farm to visit his parents. Along the way, JD's habit was to stop at a particular service station. Necessity often required me to enter the convenience store there. I walked in all clean and shiny, and walked out with my hair and clothes stinking like cigarette smoke. No matter how fast I dashed in and out of that store, the smoke still permeated everything about me and clung on until I washed it off.

> *Our minds are refreshed and our attitudes made new, as His Word washes away the influences of the world.*

For Christians walking in a polluted world, it's similar. We try not to be influenced by thoughts, attitudes, and images of the world system. Still, just because we have to walk in the environment, they invade our minds and sometimes cling to us. But, praise God, He has the answer.

> How can a young man cleanse his way?
> By taking heed according to Your word
> *(Psalm 119:9, NKJV).*

When we come to the Bible and take His Word into our hearts, He will wash us by the living water of His "rhema" Word. Our minds are refreshed and our attitudes made new as His Word washes away the influences of the world.

Your word I have hidden in my heart,
That I might not sin against You!
(Psalm 119:11, NKJV).

For whatever things were written before were written for our learning,
that we through the patience and comfort of the Scriptures might have hope
(Romans 15:4, NKJV).

> *The more Bible verses that I've made* rhema, *the more I've come to look upon sin with the same attitude as our holy and righteous God.*

Secondhand smoke was once thought to be simply an annoyance. Now we know it's hazardous to our health. What's our attitude about sin? Do we think secondhand sin does us no harm? Is the evil of the world a mere nuisance to us, or is it a real hazard to our spiritual health?

The more Bible verses that I've made *rhema*, the more I've come to look upon sin with the same attitude as our holy and righteous God. The smell of the smoke of hell can cling to us simply by beholding secondhand sin. We need to wash it off with His "rhema" Word.

Blessed are those who wash their robes, that they may have the right
to the tree of life and may go through the gates into the city
(Revelation 22:14, NIV).

We need to wash our robes so they will be without "spot or wrinkle or any such thing." If we want to be sanctified—holy and without the blemish of sin—we need to come to the fountain of His living waters and allow the Holy Spirit to wash us by the water of the "rhema" Word.

5. The "Rhema" Word is the sword of the spirit.
- Ephesians 6:17, NKJV.
"And take . . . the sword of the Spirit, which is the word ["rhema" Word] of God."

I was accustomed to thinking of the entire Bible as the "sword of the Spirit," until I studied the Greek words *logos* and *rhema*. Suddenly, I recognized that the Bible is the sheath that holds the sword. The sword of the Spirit is the particular verse we can draw from the Bible and apply as our *rhema* affirmation, saying, "It is written."

When I was young, there was a popular television program about a Spanish nobleman named Zorro. He was always fighting for the good of the people. After his daring rescues, he would draw his sword from its sheath and with three bold swipes make his mark—a "Z"—on the door or gates of the enemy.

> *The Bible is the* sheath *that holds the sword. The sword of the Spirit is the particular verse we can draw from the Bible and apply as our* rhema *affirmation, saying, "It is written."*

May I suggest that as Christians, we should be doing the same? We can be either a spiritual zero, or a spiritual Zorro. We should have God's Word hidden in our hearts so that we can pull out the sword of the Spirit and in three bold swipes—*IT . . . IS . . . WRITTEN*—leave our mark on the enemy's gates.

Let me demonstrate how we wield the sword of the Spirit. When the enemy comes against us with guilt and condemnation, we need to pull out our sword and say:

> **It is written.** I am a new creation in Christ Jesus. God is working in me to cause me to will and to act according to His good pleasure. He will complete the good work He has begun in me.[22]

When the enemy tries to cloud our minds with confusion, we need to pull out our sword and say:

> **It is written.** God is the author not of confusion, but of peace. I have not been given a spirit of fear. God has given me a spirit of power and of love and of sound mind. God is righteous. He has cut me free from the cords of the wicked.[23]

When the tempter tries to trip us and entangle our feet in his snare, we need to pull out our sword and say:

It is written. I am dead to sin, but alive to God. I am under the power of His grace, and sin shall not be my master. I have put on Christ and I will make no provision for my flesh. God has given me the victory through my Lord Jesus Christ.[24]

> *"For the word of God is living and powerful, and sharper than any two-edged sword" (Hebrews 4:12, NKJV). The word two-edged is distomon in Greek. It literally means, "two-mouthed," like a double-mouthed river.*

Now, I'd like to share a thought about God's two-edged sword mentioned in Hebrews 4:12, NKJV. A study of the Greek text revealed to me something remarkable about this familiar verse. "For the word of God is living and powerful, and sharper than any two-edged sword."

The word *two-edged* is *distomon* in Greek. It literally means, "two-mouthed," like a double-mouthed river. Please carefully consider the following excerpt from *Life Affirmations from Scripture* that the Lord inspired me to write:

He has given me the authority and eternal power of His Word.
His Word is alive, active, immovable, unshakable.
His Word is a two-edged sword—
the first edge struck when He spoke it;
the second edge strikes when I speak it.
As I speak the Word, I hear the voice of the Lord.
I am returning His Word to Him, and His Word does not return void,
but accomplishes every purpose for which He sent it.
He actively watches over His Word to make certain it is fulfilled
at the perfect time which He has appointed.
(Derived from Hebrews 4:12; Isaiah 55:9–11, 13; Jeremiah 1:12; Luke 1:20; Habakkuk 2:3.)

The Word of God becomes "two-mouthed" as we draw from His Word and confess over our lives Scriptures that have become *rhema*, alive and active within us. The blessing is not on the hearing, but on the practice of His Word. Jesus said, "Blessed rather are those who hear the word of God and obey it."[25]

If we'll apply this "two-mouthed" principle of His Word to our lives, the sword of the Spirit will cut us free from the cords of the wicked that try to bind us.[26]

6. *Rhema* increases the effectiveness of prayer.
- John 15:7 NKJV.

"If you abide in Me, and My words ["rhema" Word] abide in you, you will ask what you desire, and it shall be done for you."

I've concluded that abiding in the Word of God is the way we abide in Christ. As the entrance of His Word has increased in my heart, something amazing has transpired in my mind. God's thoughts are becoming my thoughts. His desires are becoming my desires. I want to do all things for His glory and to bring honor to His name.

When we find our delight in God, His desires become our desires. We pray according to His purposes. He hears and answers.

My prayers are no longer vain babbling. I'm asking for God's intervention according to His will that is revealed in Scripture.

> Delight yourself also in the Lord,
> and He shall give you the desires of your heart
> *(Psalm 37:4, NKJV).*

What a beautiful promise. When we find our delight in God, His desires become our desires. We pray according to His purposes. He hears and answers. Sadly, some preachers have taken this promise out of context and have twisted it to their own destruction—spawning an assembly of "name it and claim it" believers. When our delight is in the Lord, the focus of our desire is not a new Mercedes-Benz.

> Now this is the confidence that we have in Him,
> that if we ask anything **according to His will,** He hears us.
> And if we know that He hears us, whatever we ask,
> we know that we have the petitions that we have asked of Him
> *(1 John 5:14, 15. NKJV).*

God has taught me that praying His Word back to Him is the most effective way of praying according to His will. He promises to watch over His Word to perform it.[27] He also declares His Word does not return to Him void, but that it accomplishes the purposes for which He sent it.[28] Returning God's Word to Him makes us like the watchmen upon the walls:

> I have set watchmen upon your walls, O Jerusalem,
> who will never hold their peace day or night;
> you who [are His servants and by your prayers]
> put the Lord in remembrance [of His promises],
> keep not silence, and give Him no rest until
> He establishes Jerusalem and makes her a praise in the earth
> *(Isaiah 62:6, 7, AMP).*

Jesus said if we abide in Him, and His "rhema" Word abides in us, we can ask and it will be done for us according to His Word. In Luke 18, He spoke a parable about a persistent widow to show us that we ought to pray in faith and not give up. We can pray without losing heart if we know we're praying according to His Word.

As Christ concluded this parable, He exposed the burden of His heart with this sorrowful note:

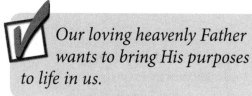

Our loving heavenly Father wants to bring His purposes to life in us.

> Nevertheless, when the Son of Man comes,
> will He really find faith on the earth?
> *(Luke 18:8, NKJV).*

Will He find faith in you? He will—if His Word has become your *rhema* affirmation.

7. No "Rhema" Word is impossible of fulfillment.

- Luke 1:37, AMP.

  "For with God nothing is ever impossible and no word ["rhema" Word] from God shall be without power or impossible of fulfillment."

- Luke 1:38, NKJV.

"Then Mary said, 'Behold the maidservant of the Lord! Let it be to me according to your word ["rhema" Word].'"

I don't mean to confuse you by using two different translations to provide sequential Scriptures. This is the only way to bring out the fullest expression of the Greek text. In the Greek, both Scriptures refer to the **"rhema" Word.**

Mary trusted God and received His Word into her heart, willingly applying it personally to her life. God blessed her because she believed that He would fulfill His Word.[29] The creative power of the Word went to work in her. God birthed His purpose in her. By His power, the Word became flesh.

> *God knows the end from the beginning, and so can we, if we'll just get into His Word where His plan is revealed.*

This is a profound thought, and I pray the Holy Spirit is working in your heart to bring understanding. It is God's desire that we recognize the creative power in His Word. He wants us to plant His Word in our hearts and let it be the word of faith that is coming from our mouth. He yearns for us to acknowledge His plan and to know who we are now that we're included in Christ. Our loving heavenly Father wants to bring His purposes to life in us.

We'll be forever changed, if we can grasp this truth: *No word of God is impossible of fulfillment.* Understanding this will create the desire to partake of His promises, to the end result that we partake of His divine nature. The identity crisis will fly out the window. We'll recognize the privilege of being called the children of God.[30]

God knows the end from the beginning, and so can we, if we'll just get into His Word where His plan is revealed. I know His plan is far greater than what I'm currently living. I trust your experience is the same. Nothing He has promised is impossible of fulfillment. We just have to depend on His power to do the work in us.

God wants you to increase the measure of your expectations; the measure you use will be measured back to you.[31]

8. It's dangerous to reject the "Rhema" Word.
- John 12:48, NKJV.

"He who rejects Me, and does not receive My words ["rhema" Word], has that which judges him—the word ["logos" Word] that I have spoken will judge him in the last day."

A loving Savior wants us to receive all that He has for us. He wants to equip us thoroughly to do His will. He wants us to depend on His power to be made perfect in our weakness. It is Almighty God who will work in you to line up your desires with His will. It is the Creator of the universe who will work in you to empower you to act. We have nothing to fear, as long as we depend on His power to walk in obedience to His Word.

My conduct reveals my attitude toward Christ and the Word of God.

That being true, I must consider this: *My conduct reveals my attitude toward Christ and the Word of God.* If I refuse to receive His Word as *rhema*—a word that I'm obeying and actively applying to my life—I'm setting myself up to have judgment pronounced against me in the last day. At the point I refuse to receive His Word and put it into practice, I am at that same point rejecting Christ.

For God did not call us to be impure, but to live a holy life.
Therefore, he who rejects this instruction does not reject man but God,
Who gives you his Holy Spirit
(1 Thessalonians 4:7, 8, NIV).

He who hears you hears Me, he who rejects you rejects Me,
and he who rejects Me rejects Him who sent Me
(Luke 10:16, NKJV).

If you've been rejecting the Word of God, I pray that the Holy Spirit is bringing you to godly sorrow and repentance. I also pray that He will prevent you from being smothered by condemnation. We know that when we confess our sins to the Lord, He is faithful and just to forgive us our sins.[32] He will blot out the record of our sins by the blood of Jesus and will remember them no more.[33] He is the God of new beginnings!

Jesus said we're blessed when we hear the "logos" Word of God and then obey and practice it.[34] This refers to hearing a commandment or promise from the Holy Bible and making it *rhema* by personally applying it. We need to recall the perfect "law of liberty" that we studied in chapter four: *We must recognize our absolute, total dependence upon Jesus Christ to perform a work in us that empowers us to walk in the commandments of God.* Then we'll walk in the law of liberty, being doers of the Word instead of just hearers, and we'll be blessed in whatever we do.[35]

Fear not, for I have redeemed you . . . I have called you by your name;
you are Mine.
When you pass through the waters, I will be with you, and through the rivers,
they will not overwhelm you. When you walk through the fire,
you will not be burned or scorched, nor will the flame kindle upon you
(Isaiah 43:1, 2, AMP).

Always remember this: *You are worth nothing less to God than the price He paid for you with the precious lifeblood of Jesus.* He will complete the good work He has begun in you. God will pour His love into your heart and empower you to love Him with all of your heart, soul, mind, and strength.[36] Even in that, you are totally dependent upon Him.

> *We must recognize our absolute, total dependence upon Jesus Christ to perform a work in us that empowers us to walk in the commandments of God.*

He wants you to come to Him in faith—earnestly seeking Him. He will reward you beyond your wildest dreams. By the creative power of His Word and the dynamite power of the Holy Spirit at work within you, He will **cause** you to be all that He has **called** you to be.

This is my prayer for you:

That He would grant you, according to the riches of His glory, to be strengthened with might through His Spirit in the inner man, that Christ may dwell in your hearts through faith; that you, being rooted and grounded in love, may be able to comprehend with all the saints what is the width and length and depth and height—to know the love of Christ which passes knowledge; that you may be filled with all the fullness of God (Ephesians 3:16–19, NKJV).

Now to Him who is able to do exceedingly abundantly above all that we ask or think, according to the power that works in us, to Him be glory in the church by Christ Jesus to all generations, forever and ever. Amen (Ephesians 3:20, NKJV).

The power of "I am"

The Holy Spirit first poured *Life Affirmations from Scripture* into my heart in 1996 when I was sitting in a hotel room in Houston, Texas. As He led me into this process of taking God's Word and making it my *rhema* utterance, I was uneasy about something. I noticed many of the affirmations began with the words. *I am.* It seemed that I was assuming something, and it made me very uncomfortable to speak in that way.

Suddenly, I was impressed to say, "I am who God says I am!" Still, I was uneasy speaking the affirmations in the form it seemed that He had given me. Then the Lord led me to Romans 4:17, "God who gives life to the dead and calls things that are not as though they were. . . ."

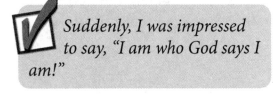

Suddenly, I was impressed to say, "I am who God says I am!"

His Word says I am predestined to become like His Son.[37] I'm not there yet. But God, the One who knows the end from the beginning, counts it as done. Who am I to argue with God?

I think the reason the Lord led me to speak the affirmations aloud is because faith comes by hearing, and I needed to hear it by my own voice. Without faith, I can't please my heavenly Father.

The next thought impressed on me was much deeper. I knew it had to be the leading of the Spirit, because I was astonished at the concept. It required much prayer and reflection for me to accept it. As I now share this with you, I encourage you to receive it in the same prayerful attitude.

Let me first establish the foundation for understanding. When God told Moses that He was sending him to deliver the Israelites out of Egypt, Moses wanted to know God's name for reference. We find the record of this conversation in Exodus 3:13, 14.

> Then Moses said to God, "Indeed, when I come to the children of Israel and say to them, 'The God of your fathers has sent me to you,' and they say to me, 'What is His name?' what shall I say to them?"
>
> And God said to Moses, "I AM WHO I AM." And He said, "Thus you shall say to the children of Israel, 'I AM has sent me to you' " (NKJV).

God proclaimed His name as "I AM." Such a declaration reveals that God is not dependent upon any power but His own. He is almighty and all-sufficient. Maybe that's why I was uneasy to affirm the "I am" statements. But the Spirit of the Lord led me into a deeper understanding of God's purpose in beginning my *rhema* utterances. At the same time, I came into a deeper appreciation for the commandment of not taking the Lord's name in vain.

> *Any time we speak the words "I am," we should be cautious about the declaration that follows.*

I was led to understand that any time we speak the words *I am,* we should be cautious about the declaration that follows. If we declare something that is not scriptural—for example, "I am without hope"—we are, in a sense, taking the Lord's name in vain. On the other hand, when we proclaim "I am" and follow it with an affirmation that is from Scripture, we are saying, in essence: "By God's grace, I am who God says I am." It demonstrates that we believe His testimony, and it brings Him glory.

The apostle Paul said it best, "But by the grace of God I am what I am, and His grace toward me was not in vain."[38] Once I gained that same understanding, I was excited to speak the affirmations over my life just as God had given them to me. And I considered them accomplished in His eyes, *calling things that had not yet been revealed to me by physical evidence as though they already existed.*[39] Isn't this the very essence of faith—being sure of what we hope for and certain of what we do not yet see?[40]

Distilled wisdom

We started this study of *rhema* affirmations in chapter seven by noting that miracles followed the authority of the words of Christ. We've labored through a lot of teaching in two chapters, just to prove the authority that His Word should exercise in our lives. It's not important that you remember the Greek words *logos* or *rhema*. It's not important that you recall the difference between *claiming a promise* and *speaking an affirmation*. What's important to remember is this:

- Confessing God's Word with your living voice will increase your faith.
- God's Word is life to you—it's your spiritual nutrition.

- Christ will sustain and uphold you by His Word, if it's in your heart and mouth.
- The Word of God will wash away the influences of the world's system.
- The "sword of the Spirit" is the Word that you are applying personally.
- Return God's Word to Him when you pray—it increases the power of your prayers.
- No Word of God is impossible of fulfillment.
- An apathetic attitude toward God's Word is a dangerous heart condition.
- Miracles from God follow the authority of His Word.
- Increase the measure of your expectancy—the measure you use will be measured back to you.

References

1. Psalm 34:8, NKJV.
2. Hebrews 6:5, NIV.
3. 2 Peter 1:3.
4. Isaiah 7:9, NIV.
5. Hebrews 6:4, 5.
6. 2 Corinthians 6:14.
7. Acts 5:32.
8. 2 Corinthians 12:9.
9. Philippians 3:14.
10. Philippians 1:6.
11. Isaiah 46:10; Ephesians 1:11.
12. Romans 4:17.
13. Galatians 4:19.
14. John 10:10.
15. Revelation 12:11.
16. Revelation 3:20, NKJV.
17. 1 Kings 19:12.
18. Hebrews 12:2.
19. Isaiah 50:4.
20. Romans 15:13.
21. James 1:5–8, NKJV.
22. 2 Corinthians 5:17; Philippians 2:13; 1:6.
23. 1 Corinthians 14:33; 2 Timothy 1:7; Psalm 129:4.
24. Romans 6:11, 14; 13:14; 1 Corinthians 15:57.
25. Luke 11:28, NIV.
26. Psalm 129:4.
27. Jeremiah 1:12.
28. Isaiah 55:11.
29. Luke 1:45.
30. 1 John 3:1.
31. Luke 6:38.
32. 1 John 1:9.
33. Hebrews 10:17.
34. Luke 11:28.
35. James 1:25, NKJV.
36. Romans 5:5; Mark 12:30.
37. Romans 8:29.
38. 1 Corinthians 15:10, NKJV.
39. Romans 4:17.
40. Hebrews 11:1.

Chapter Nine
The Last Word

Picture this: you're seated at a table centered on an elevated stage in view of an audience of thousands. An old man, disheveled in appearance, shuffles across the stage and takes a seat next to you. The debate is about to begin. The moderator calls on the elderly man to speak first. He speaks with great authority and factual evidence on the theory of gravity. Now, it's your turn to talk.

Clearing your throat, you begin, "While all of this man's teaching sounds impressive, I don't believe it can be proven. It can't be seen. There's no real proof. This information is outdated. How can we know for certain? I really don't think . . ."

The debate goes on. Your position is uninformed, but fixed. His words are beyond your comprehension. Who do you think would win this debate—you or Albert Einstein, the physicist and genius Nobel prizewinner?

There's something peculiar about human nature. We love to be right, don't we? If we've formed an opinion on a particular topic, we defend it with all of our might and dismiss anyone who challenges our ideas. Let's face it. We can be stubborn as a mule when we just "know" we're right about something.

I've always had an intense longing for God. Years of anxious Bible study left me without a clear explanation of His plan. In seeking understanding from other Christians, I was unsatisfied with their answers. When it comes to the heavenly banquet laid out in the Word of God, most of us eat little more than crumbs from His table. Since we've been taught not to speak with our mouth full, I guess we choose not to eat His Word while we're so busy expressing our ideas.

Like Nicodemus, most of us debate with the Lord. He offers a feast of wisdom. We offer leftovers of human reasoning.

Seek the Lord while He may be found, Call upon Him while He is near.
Let the wicked forsake his way, And the unrighteous man his thoughts;
Let him return to the Lord, And He will have mercy on him;
And to our God, For He will abundantly pardon.

"For My thoughts are not your thoughts,
Nor are your ways My ways," says the Lord.

"For as the heavens are higher than the earth,
So are My ways higher than your ways,
And My thoughts than your thoughts."
(Isaiah 55:6–9, NKJV).

I believe every human in the world suffers from an inward emptiness until he or she develops an intimate relationship with the Lord. God designed us to be filled with His Spirit of life. He created us in His image,[1] to participate in His divine nature and mind. There's a void in us that only God can fill. Some people try packing all the wrong stuff into their barren lives and wonder why they can't find true peace and joy. Others recognize that only God can satisfy their emptiness, but they just don't know how to be filled with Him.

I meet many who have accepted Christ as their Savior, but who have rejected His Lordship. Some poor souls, walking in "religion" instead of "relationship," are completely unaware of their condition. This is dangerous. Ignorance is not bliss.

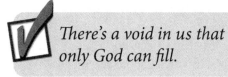

There's a void in us that only God can fill.

Others realize something is missing and anxiously struggle to change their condition. This, too, can be dangerous. The struggle can strengthen us, but the anxiety is harmful. We all need to have the assurance of God's promises. We need to appreciate His plan for our lives and the power we find when walking in surrender to Him.

If we're arguing against the wisdom of God, we won't win. The debate must be ended. What we need is increased faith. *If our faith is little, we expect little.* A loving God is calling us closer to Him. I believe we want to draw nearer—but how do we do this? There's only one solution for silencing the inward struggle of human reasoning and drawing near to God in faith. We have to go deeper into the sweet water of the Lord.

The sweet healing waters

In the Old Testament, Ezekiel 47, we find the record of a vision God gave His prophet. In this vision, the Lord showed Ezekiel water flowing from the temple. Ezekiel was led through the water. At first, it was ankle-deep. Then, knee-deep. Soon the water was up to his waist. Finally, the water became deep enough to swim in—a river so vast that no one could cross it.

In the Bible, water symbolizes two things: The Holy Spirit of God[2] and the Word of God.[3] In this vision, God was revealing to Ezekiel the depths of knowledge that could be found in Him. The farther we go into His sweet, healing waters, the more we are refreshed and regenerated. The deeper we go into God's Word, the more the Holy Spirit brings understanding and power into our lives. The debate of human reasoning is ended.

> For "who has known the mind of the Lord that he may instruct Him?"
> But we have the mind of Christ.
> *(1 Corinthians 2:16, NKJV).*

The mind of Christ. We need it. We want it. It's offered as a gift, and we should line up to receive it. If we had the mind of Christ, we would understand God's plan. The old routine of "three steps forward, two steps back" would halt. Jesus said our lukewarm condition repulsed Him to the point He would like to spew us out of His mouth. I've known Christians, and I include myself in this category, who've been likewise disgusted by their state of being hot one day and cold the next. The blending of these two conditions is so distastefully lukewarm that we are ready to spit it out.

God endowed His Word with life-giving power, a creative power that reproduces the mind of Christ in us.

We have been given the mind of Christ, but we're not drawing on it as we should. His thoughts and His Wisdom are recorded in the Bible. The Word of God is the mind of Christ, the healing water, the source of life. Some of us dip our toes into the water. Some wade in ankle-deep. There are those who venture in knee-deep, and a number who have gone in up to their waist. Oh, but God wants us to take the plunge and swim in His river of healing waters! When we step out into the depths of His mind, the Spirit and the Word will become our spiritual "inner-tube," supporting us throughout life in absolute dependence upon the Lord.

God endowed His Word with life-giving power, a creative power that reproduces the mind of Christ in us.[4] As we begin to plant God's Word in our hearts and speak it with our mouths, we'll be changed. He will cause us to operate under the influence of His understanding. He plugs us in to His power source and gives us the strength we lack. His power lightens the lamp of understanding,[5] keeping us fully charged and energized to walk by faith. He said to us:

My grace is sufficient for you,
for My power is made perfect in weakness
(2 Corinthians 12:9, NIV).

My heavenly Father had to allow me to reach the edge of destruction before He could teach me absolute dependence upon His love and power. I cried out in my trouble and He delivered me. He sent His Word and healed me.[6] I am the redeemed of the Lord.[7] I no longer dispute His testimony of who I am "in Christ." It was a hard lesson to go through. He escorted me over difficult terrain, all the while cradling me in His love. Oh, how sweet the victory when He thrust out the doubt and disbelief of the enemy.

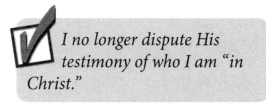

I no longer dispute His testimony of who I am "in Christ."

The eternal God is your refuge,
And underneath are the everlasting arms;
He will thrust out the enemy from before you,
And will say, "Destroy!"
(Deuteronomy 33:27, NKJV).

A cup of water

I tell you the truth, anyone who gives you a cup of water in my name
because you belong to Christ will certainly not lose his reward
(Mark 9:41, NIV).

That's what I'm doing in this book—sharing a cup of the healing waters of His Word with you. I've been rewarded greatly through this assignment. I praise God for teaching me to exalt His Word and empowering me to share it.

First, He caused me to be still and know that He is God. He sat me down at the roar of His waterfalls, and I drank from His fountain of living water.

As soon as I accepted the Lord's call to ministry, He kept me at His feet for months on end to learn from Him. In fact, this thought was impressed upon my mind: *Forget what you think you know and come sit at My feet. I will teach you from My Word.*

I hope to write about this experience some day soon, because this was when I really learned to exalt His Word over my "religious" opinions. This was how God ordered my steps and led me into the Seventh-day Adventist Church. Let me share a few highlights.

The Lord started me on an exhaustive study of the old and new covenants. He opened my eyes to the truth that His Ten Commandments are eternal. I had previously been taught they were nailed to the cross and just hadn't personally studied on that topic.

It was made so clear to me in Scripture, I didn't have a problem accepting this truth.

God said, "Forget what you think you know and come sit at My feet. I will teach you from My Word."

Of course, there remained a "doctrine of men" plank in my eye. I had to ask, *What about the Sabbath, Lord?* After examining all the Scriptures on His wonderful Sabbath truth, I became a joyful celebrator of His seventh-day Sabbath. This change increased my understanding of the true "law of liberty." It wasn't until I started celebrating the Lord's day, His seventh-day Sabbath, that I learned to depend on Him for sanctification and understood true freedom from performance.

You might recall that in chapter three I mentioned the amusing irony of my appearances on 3ABN. God had to turn me 180 degrees before He could open that door. I was a Sabbath celebrator for nearly two years, and I still wouldn't watch this network, because I knew it was run by Adventists.

My "religious" pride prevented me from tuning in—because I had heard some disparaging remarks about the beliefs of Adventists. But one day, by divine providence, I landed on the 3ABN channel. I was astonished. They were teaching the same Bible truths that I had grown to appreciate from the increased understanding God had given me. Plus, this channel was presenting truth I desperately needed—a scriptural understanding of prophecy.

After a few months of viewing 3ABN programming, I realized Adventists had been given a "bad rap." These folks were teaching more Bible truths than any other denomination I knew. I started attending an Adventist church in my area and became a member on June 8, 2002. Six months later, God opened the door for my first appearance on 3ABN.

Exalting His Word has changed my Christian experience and my life. I don't think I fully appreciated all that God had done in me until I sat down to write this book.

The experience has been amazing. In the past, several people had encouraged me to write a book. I know any talent I have is a gift from the Lord, so my standard reply was, "I will not write unless it's for God's glory." This comment from long ago had slipped my memory. As I completed the last chapter, the Lord reminded me. He had taken note of my reply and honored my desire to bring Him glory.

God has been preparing me for years to record this teaching. He wouldn't let me write it until I was living it on a consistent basis and had gained increased understanding. Although I self-published *Life Affirmations from Scripture* in 1999, it was more of a devotional writing of compiled verses. I consider what you hold in your hands to be the first real book God has given me to write. It has been such a joy to write this for you. In the process, God has demonstrated to me the power of His Word and leading of His Spirit, as well as the wisdom of committing my plans to Him for His glory.

Commit to the Lord whatever you do,
and your plans will succeed
(Proverbs 16:3, NIV).

From my perspective, God has performed a miracle to accomplish this project through a novice. In wide-eyed wonderment, I marvel at how He ordered my steps[8] and enabled me to complete this book in less than three weeks. I say this for His glory. To top it off, the Lord provided me with a professional proofreader as an assistant.

Pat Mudgett, the organizer of the first Word Warrior Squadron (Berkeley Springs, West Virginia), volunteered to proofread the manuscript for me. I've only known Pat for a few months. I'm so thankful that God placed such an enthusiastic helper in my life. Her loving support and devotion of time have been a true blessing from the Lord. I'm grateful to Pat and my precious husband; my sister; my Santa Anna, Texas, church family; and all the others who have lovingly held me up in prayer.

I'm often guilty of the sin of procrastination, but writing this book was an exception. A busy speaking schedule, mechanical failure of my computer, personal illness, and various family emergencies gobbled up the time I scheduled for writing. It seemed there was an assignment from the camp of the enemy sent against me to prevent this book from being completed. However, greater is He who is in me than he who is in the world.[9]

As the deadline loomed, I knew I had to be surrendered and totally dependent upon the Lord to accomplish the task. I confess to feeling painfully inadequate to take His divine thoughts and place them before you with my limited speech—especially in such a short time. I think the Lord allowed me to get into such a time constraint so that I wouldn't rely on myself, but on Him.[10] He wanted to prove, once again, it's all about Him and not about me. Glory to God—He did!

At the cruel cross of Calvary, God lavished His love on you and me.

God blessed me in the process of this writing. I came to appreciate how alive and active His Word really is.[11] The mind of Christ has been given to us, just as His Word promises. And He wants to give us even more. He is calling us into the depth of His living water.

Sanctified minds

"Sanctify them by Your truth. Your word is truth."[12] This was Christ's prayer just before He entered the Garden of Gethsemane. He faced the hour of His passion at Calvary with eyes fixed on His holy and righteous Father and His heart focused on us. He prayed that the Word of God would make us holy, because

Without holiness no one will see the Lord
(Hebrews 12:14, NIV).

He prayed according to God's will. He knew His prayer was heard and answered and that God **would** make us holy by the creative power of His Word. Satisfied, Christ pressed on to fulfill the plan of His passion, offering Himself up as the sacrifice for our sins.[13] At the cruel cross of Calvary, God lavished His love on you and me.

But God demonstrates His own love toward us,
in that while we were still sinners, Christ died for us
(Romans 5:8, NKJV).

To win the hearts of sinners, He gave His all. Why do we think He would do anything less for us now that we've become His children?[14] An all-loving, all-powerful God is willing to do all things in us, for us, and through us. He yearns for us to draw on His power. He longs for us to come and partake of His promises. God has included us "in Christ" as co-heirs with His Son.[15] He positioned us "in Christ." If we're abiding in Christ, we're lined up to receive the blessings that flow from the head of His Son to each member of His body, the church.

> It is because of him that you are in Christ Jesus,
> who has become for us wisdom from God—
> that is, our righteousness, holiness and redemption
> *(1 Corinthians 1:30, NIV).*

> For no matter how many promises God has made, they are "Yes" in Christ.
> And so through him the "Amen" is spoken by us to the glory of God
> *(2 Corinthians 1:20, NIV).*

> It is God who works in you
> to will and to act according to his good purpose
> *(Philippians 2:13, NIV).*

> I know whom I have believed and am persuaded
> that He is able to keep what I have committed to Him until that Day
> *(2 Timothy 1:12, NKJV).*

What more could we ask for? Christ paid the ultimate price to redeem us from sin.[16] God includes us in Christ, when we accept His gift of salvation by grace. We can partake of all of His promises. His Word and His Spirit work in us, to empower us to walk in God's will.

God vows to complete the good work He has begun in us.

Above all, God vows to complete the good work He has begun in us[17]—that is, if we'll simply give Him permission to do this, by cooperating with Him. We must quit leaning on human understanding and start leaning on His Word.[18]

What are we exalting?

The Bible declares there are only two kinds of wisdom—heavenly and demonic (see James 3:13–18). We're instructed to gain understanding of God's righteous way of doing all things. We're also counseled to demonstrate understanding by our good works, done with humility.

What does this tell us? It tells me we should be seeking the mind of Christ from the Word of God. And we should be walking in the humility of Christ, led by the Spirit of love and holiness.

We must quit leaning on human understanding and start leaning on His Word.

The theme text for my 3ABN program series, *Exalting His Word,* and for this book comes from Psalm 138:2. It reveals that God exalts His name and His Word above all else, and that **He exalts His Word even above His name.** The Lord gave me this Scripture as a banner over the ministry He has entrusted to me. God wants to raise up "Word Warriors" to complete His work on earth, for the soon return of Christ.

When Scripture says God exalts His Word above all else, it means He has assigned it the highest rank of importance. He causes His life-giving, creative Word to be more powerful than any other force. Because His living Word, Jesus Christ, has perfected obedience to His will, God magnifies and glorifies His Word to the highest place of praise. Every knee will bow to His Word, Jesus Christ.

What are we exalting? To what do we bow our knees? Do we still lean on our own understanding, instead of the wisdom of God?

What we exalt is *revealed* by our attitudes, our thoughts, and the words that escape from our mouths. What we exalt is *demonstrated* by our actions and conduct.

What *proves* whether we exalt human reasoning or the mind of Christ is this: The measure of obedience and faith in which we walk.

Increase the measure of your expectancy

Perhaps you're familiar with a little book, *The Prayer of Jabez,* that made quite a stir in the Christian community not long ago. When it was first published, I was flooded with copies sent from people who had been attending my meetings. So many thought I would enjoy reading it, because it was similar to the message I had been sharing for over eight months.

The Lord had earlier impressed this thought on me: *Teach My people to increase the measure of their expectations. The measure they use will be measured back to them.*[19]

> "Teach My people to increase the measure of their expectations. The measure they use will be measured back to them."

I only know one way to teach this. I encourage everyone to get into His Word and know Him for who He is. The Word is the answer for overcoming our crisis of identity and learning who we are "in Christ." The Word of God reveals His plan for our lives. It is essential that we earnestly seek Him and exalt His Word above all else.

"For I know the plans I have for you," declares the LORD,
"plans to prosper you and not to harm you, plans to give you hope and a future.
Then you will call upon Me and come and pray to Me, and I will listen to you.
You will seek Me and find Me when you seek Me with all your heart.
I will be found by you," declares the LORD, "and will bring you back from
captivity"
(Jeremiah 29:11–14, NIV).

Are we always mindful that our destiny is to become like Jesus?[20] We are meant to be partakers of His divine nature.[21] We can't complete the work by human effort; we need His Spirit.[22] Christ's power will be made perfect in our weakness, if we learn to depend totally on Him. We can trust our loving God. Everything He does in our lives is for our ***eternal*** benefit.

The LORD has appeared . . . saying:
"Yes, I have loved you with an everlasting love;
Therefore with lovingkindness I have drawn you. . . .
Call to Me, and I will answer you, and show you
great and mighty things, which you do not know"
(Jeremiah 31:3; 33:3, NKJV).

Aren't we wearied by our limited expectations? God wants to fill us with love, joy, peace, and expectant hope in His promises. He wants to fill us with His power. This will happen only if we give Him permission to work in us and cause us to exalt His Word. In His Word, we'll find salvation and righteousness—from faith to faith.

> For I am not ashamed of the gospel of Christ,
> for it is the power of God to salvation for everyone who believes . . .
> For in it the righteousness of God is revealed from faith to faith;
> as it is written, "The just shall live by faith"
> *(Romans 1:16, 17, NKJV).*

His Word is final

"For I am the LORD, I do not change." "Jesus Christ is the same yesterday, today, and forever."[23] The Word who created the entire universe also created you. His passion over you is great. He died so you could have life. We don't have to be fearful in approaching the Lord. We love Him because He first loved us.[24]

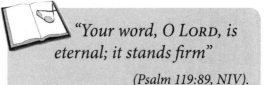

"Your word, O LORD, is eternal; it stands firm"

(Psalm 119:89, NIV).

He wants to save us from our limited human reasoning and our self-destructive behavior. He desires to give us an abundant life now, and a life of indescribable glory throughout eternity.[25]

Why would we neglect so great a salvation? How will we escape if we ignore His plan?[26] We don't have to wonder what His will is—**it is written.** It is also written, "Your word, O LORD, is eternal; it stands firm."[27]

> He was clothed with a robe dipped in blood,
> and His name is called The Word of God.
> Do not be afraid; I am the First and the Last
> *(Revelation 19:13; 1:17, NKJV).*

His Word was the beginning of all things. Everything we know came into existence by the Word of God.[28] The miracle of creation is wrapped inside His Word. All of your potential is wrapped inside His Word.

His Word is final. It cannot be altered. He is the God of His Word, and He does not change. We can have absolute trust in His loving-kindness. His love endures forever.[29] We can have absolute faith that His Word does not return to Him empty.[30] It's true, God watches over His Word to perform it.[31]

I pray that God will give you an unquenchable desire for His Word. I pray He will raise you up as a "Word Warrior" and empower you to walk as Jesus walked.[32] I pray He will multiply His mercy, love, and grace to you.

Hear the heart of a loving Father, saying, "Come—exalt My Word!"

> I will confess and praise You [O God] with my whole heart. . . .
> I will worship toward Your holy temple, and praise Your name
> for Your loving-kindness and for Your truth and faithfulness;
> for You have exalted above all else Your name and Your word
> and You have magnified Your word above all Your name!
> *(Psalm 138:1, 2, AMP).*

References

1. Genesis 1:27; Colossians 3:10.
2. John 7:38.
3. Ephesians 5:26.
4. Colossians 3:10.
5. 2 Samuel 22:29.
6. Psalm 107:20.
7. Psalm 107:2.
8. Psalm 37:23.
9. 1 John 4:4.
10. 2 Corinthians 1:9.
11. Hebrews 4:12.
12. John 17:17, NKJV.
13. Ephesians 5:2; Hebrews 10:12.
14. Romans 8:32.
15. Romans 8:17.
16. 1 Peter 1:18, 19.
17. Philippians 1:6.
18. Proverbs 3:5.
19. Mark 4:24; Luke 6:37, 38.
20. Romans 8:29.
21. 2 Peter 1:4.
22. Galatians 3:3.
23. Malachi 3:6; Hebrews 13:8, NKJV.
24. 1 John 4:19.
25. John 10:10; Ephesians 1:18.
26. Hebrews 2:3.
27. Psalm 119:89, NIV.
28. John 1:3.
29. Psalm 107:1.
30. Isaiah 55:11.
31. Jeremiah 1:12.
32. 1 John 2:6.

Appendix
Life Affirmations From Scripture

Instructions: Life Affirmations From Scripture

I challenge you to set aside time each day for the next month and speak life affirmations from Scripture aloud. No matter how well you know the Scriptures—or how long you've been serving the Lord—I believe you'll find you are tapping into a spiritual power source like none other you have known before.

Here are some suggestions that I've found helpful:

1. **Devote thirty minutes** each day to this practice of meditating on God's Word. I've learned my days go much smoother when I dedicate time early in the morning. If you can't squeeze thirty minutes into your schedule in a single time slot, try dividing this practice into two fifteen-minute segments—or three ten-minute exercises.

2. **Begin with prayer.** Ask God to sanctify you by His Word (see John 17:17). Ask Him to teach you His will. Ask to be filled with His Spirit and for the Holy Spirit to be your teacher. I incorporate the speaking of affirmations into my regular prayer time. This whole practice is a process of prayer. After some rehearsal, many Christians realize a spontaneous burst of praise arises in their hearts. Most have mentioned a new level of intimacy they experience in their prayer time through this process.

3. **Speak the affirmation and supporting Scriptures aloud.** As you speak the affirmation (the words within the box), you're returning God's Word to Him. When I speak the supporting Scriptures aloud, I sense I'm hearing the voice of God. Scripture is His Word.

4. **Repeat the affirmation** after saying the Scriptures. Change the wording, if necessary, to offer direct thanksgiving to God.

5. **Conclude with prayer and praise.** Thank God for watching over His Word to perform it. Thank Him for making known "the end from the beginning." Most of all, thank Him that He calls things that are not as though they already were.

6. Be consistent. If you're like me, you may feel a little uneasy about speaking some of these promises in the affirmation form at first. In the beginning, I felt like a hypocrite when I heard my living voice saying these things; I knew what I was speaking didn't match my experience. I was speaking things that were not yet evident to my physical senses as though they already existed. That's exactly what God does; He counts them accomplished. Praise the Lord, we can accept His testimony about us as being something He will work in us, causing us to be all that He has called us to be.

7. Repeat. When you've completed this entire segment, simply start over again. Each time you repeat an affirmation, it becomes more alive in you. God's Word cannot be exhausted.

Note: All bold type in these texts is emphasis supplied by the author.

The following affirmations are an excerpt from the book

Life Affirmations From Scripture

by
Shelley Quinn

1. God Has a Plan—Seek Him

Heavenly Father, I am seeking You with all of my heart.

Teach me how to draw nearer to You. Teach me how to "press in" to Your presence.

You have loved me with an everlasting love. Help me to accept Your love.

You have a plan for my life, and it's better than the one I'm living.

I have only this lifetime to prepare for eternity. I realize my choices can have eternal consequences. Please cause me to make the right choices.

Teach me Your will. Reveal to me the path I should walk to find joy in Your presence.

Cause me to seek You earnestly. Cause me to trust in Your Word.

Psalm 63:1–4, NIV

O God, you are my God, earnestly I seek you; my soul thirsts for you . . . my body longs for you, in a dry and weary land where there is no water. I have seen you in the sanctuary and beheld your power and your glory. Because your love is better than life, my lips will glorify you. I will praise you as long as I live, and in your name I will lift up my hands.

Jeremiah 31:3, NKJV

The LORD has appeared of old to me, saying: "Yes, I have loved you with an everlasting love; Therefore with lovingkindness I have drawn you."

Jeremiah 29:11–14, NIV

"For I know the plans I have for you," declares the LORD, "plans to prosper you and not to harm you, plans to give you hope and a future. Then you will call upon me and come and pray to me, and I will listen to you. You will seek me and find me when you seek me with all your heart. I will be found by you," declares the LORD, "and will bring you back from captivity."

Deuteronomy 30:19, 20, NKJV

I have set before you life and death, blessing and cursing; therefore choose life . . . that you may love the LORD your God, that you may obey His voice, and that you may cling to Him, for He is your life.

Psalm 16:11, NKJV

You will show me the path of life; in Your presence is fullness of joy; at Your right hand are pleasures forevermore.

Isaiah 48:17, NIV

I am the LORD your God, who teaches you what is best for you, who directs you in the way you should go.

Proverbs 3:5, 6, NKJV

Trust in the LORD with all your heart, and lean not on your own understanding; In all your ways acknowledge Him, and He shall direct your paths.

2. The Word Lights the Way

His Word illuminates the pathway for my life. His Words are not idle—they bring and sustain life. God has revealed His plan for me, making known the end from the beginning.

Speaking the Word lets me hear it with my living voice (and faith comes by hearing).

My spoken affirmation develops "faith actions" as I let His Word do a work within me.

I am "chosen" to be obedient to Christ, through the sanctifying power of the Holy Spirit and of the Word of God.

Meditating on His Word is the most valuable investment of my time. Time is life! How I invest my time is how I invest my life!

Psalm 119:105; Proverbs 6:23, NKJV

Your word is a lamp to my feet and a light to my path. . . . For the commandment is a lamp, and the law a light.

Deuteronomy 32:46, 47, NIV

Take to heart all the words I have solemnly declared to you this day. They are not just idle words for you—**they are your life.**

Hebrews 1:3, AMP

He [Jesus] is the sole expression of the glory of God . . . and He is the perfect imprint and very image of [God's] nature, **upholding** and **maintaining** and **guiding** and **propelling** the universe **by His mighty word of power.**

Isaiah 46:10, NIV

I make known the end from the beginning, from ancient times, what is still to come.

Romans 10:10, 17, NKJV

For with the heart one believes unto righteousness, and with the mouth **confession is made unto salvation.** . . . So then faith comes by hearing, and hearing by the word of God.

James 2:17, NIV

Faith by itself, if it is not accompanied by action, is dead.

1 Peter 1:2, AMP

Who were **chosen** and foreknown by God the Father and consecrated (sanctified, made holy) by the Spirit **to be obedient** to Jesus Christ.

John 17:17, NKJV

Sanctify them by Your truth. Your Word is truth.

Psalm 19:14, NIV

May the words of my mouth and the meditation of my heart be pleasing in your sight, O LORD, my Rock and my Redeemer.

3. Let the Word Dwell in You—All of His Promises Are Yours

I let His Word dwell in me richly that I might possess His knowledge and wisdom. I want the mind of Christ operating through me. I trust God to watch over His Word to perform it. I am confident that Almighty God has the power to accomplish everything He has promised.

All of God's promises are mine through Christ Jesus and my obedience to Him.

I regard and call God's promises that are not yet physically apparent as if they were already brought into existence.

Colossians 3:16, NKJV

Let the word of Christ dwell in you richly in all wisdom, teaching and admonishing one another.

1 Corinthians 1:30, NKJV

But of Him you are in Christ Jesus, who became for us wisdom from God.

1 Corinthians 2:16, NKJV

For "who has known the mind of the LORD that he may instruct Him?" But we have the mind of Christ.

Jeremiah 1:12, NIV

The LORD said to me, ". . . I am watching to see that my word is fulfilled."

1 Kings 8:24, NKJV

You have kept what You promised . . .; You have both spoken with Your mouth and fulfilled it with Your hand.

Romans 4:20, 21, NKJV

He did not waver at the promise of God through unbelief, but was strengthened in faith, giving glory to God, and being fully convinced that what He had promised He was also able to perform.

2 Corinthians 1:20, NIV

For no matter how many promises God has made, they are "Yes" in Christ. And so through him the "Amen" is spoken by us to the glory of God.

Hebrews 10:35–39, NKJV

Therefore do not cast away your confidence, which has great reward. For you have need of endurance, so that after you have done the will of God, you may receive the promise.

Romans 4:17, NKJV

God, who gives life to the dead and calls those things which do not exist as though they did.

4. Born-Again Seed Potential

I am born-again by the life-giving and everlasting Word of God, and the power of His Spirit. Almighty God is my "Abba," Father.

His Word is incorruptible seed. The potential of any harvest is in the seed. All my potential is wrapped inside His seed—His holy Word.

John 3:5–7, NIV

I tell you the truth, no one can enter the kingdom of God unless he is born of water and the Spirit. Flesh gives birth to flesh, but the Spirit gives birth to spirit. You should not be surprised at my saying, "You must be born again."

1 Peter 1:22, 23, NKJV

Since you have purified your souls in obeying the truth through the Spirit . . . having been born again, not of corruptible seed but incorruptible, through the word of God which lives and abides forever.

Luke 8:11, NIV

This is the meaning of the parable: The seed is the word of God.

James 1:18, 21, AMP

And it was of His own [free] will that **He gave us birth . . . by [His] Word of Truth.** . . . So get rid of all uncleanness and the rampant outgrowth of wickedness, and in a humble (gentle, modest) spirit receive and welcome the Word which implanted and rooted [in your hearts] contains the power to save your souls.

5. A New Creation in Christ—Release the Past

I am a new creation in Christ Jesus. I do not dwell on the past, for God is doing a new thing in me. I release my past and press forward. My old nature has vanished; now only my new Christlike nature exists.

2 Corinthians 5:17, NKJV

Therefore, if anyone is in Christ, he is a new creation; old things have passed away; behold, all things have become new.

Isaiah 43:18, 19, NIV

Forget the former things; do not dwell on the past. See, I am doing a new thing! Now it springs up; do you not perceive it?"

Philippians 3:13, 14, NIV

I do not consider myself yet to have taken hold of it. But one thing I do: Forgetting what is behind and straining toward what is ahead, I press on toward the goal to win the prize for which God has called me heavenward in Christ Jesus.

6. Positioned "in Christ"

I am positioned "in Christ Jesus." Because I have received Christ as my Savior, I now have a spiritual union with Him. The "law of the Spirit of life" works in me.

When I look into the Word of God, I begin to see a vision—a reflection—of who I am in Christ. When I think and act according to the Word, I am blessed in whatever I do.

Ephesians 1:13, 14, NIV

And **you also were included in Christ** when you heard the word of truth, the gospel of your salvation. Having believed, you were marked in him with a seal, the promised Holy Spirit, who is a deposit guaranteeing our inheritance until the redemption of those who are God's possession.

1 Corinthians 1:30, AMP

But it is from Him that you have your life **in Christ Jesus**, whom God has made **our Wisdom** from God . . . **our Righteousness** . . . putting us in right standing with God, and **our Consecration**—making us pure and holy; and **our Redemption**—providing our ransom from eternal penalty for sin.

1 Corinthians 6:17, NKJV

But he who is joined to the LORD is one spirit with Him.

Romans 7:23–25; 8:2, AMP

But I discern in my bodily members—in the sensitive appetites and wills of the flesh—a **different law** (rule of action) at war against the law of my mind . . . and making me a prisoner to the **law of sin.** . . . Who will release and deliver me from [the shackles of] this body of death? O thank God!—He will! through Jesus Christ . . . our LORD! . . . For the **law of the Spirit of life** [which is] in Christ Jesus [the law of our new being] has freed me from the **law of sin** and of death.

James 1:23–25, NIV

Anyone who listens to the word but does not do what it says is like a man who **looks at his face in a mirror** and, after looking at himself, goes away and immediately forgets what he looks like. But the man who looks intently into the perfect law that gives freedom, and continues to do this, not forgetting what he has heard, but doing it—he will be blessed in what he does.

7. Redeemed and Saved by God's Grace

I am the redeemed of the Lord, saved by His marvelous grace.

Nothing I could do could earn or merit His superabundant favor; it is purely a gift of grace from the Lord.

Thank You, Lord Jesus, for redeeming me. I know I could never save myself!

Thank You, Father, for Your gracious gift of life!

Psalm 107:2, NKJV

Let the redeemed of the LORD say so.

Galatians 3:10, 13, AMP

And all who depend on the Law—who are seeking to be justified by obedience to the **law of rituals**—are under a curse and doomed to disappointment and destruction; for it is written in the Scriptures, Cursed . . . be everyone who does not continue to abide (live and remain) by all the precepts and commands written in the **book of the Law,** and practice them. . . . **Christ purchased our freedom** (redeeming us) from the curse (doom) of the Law's (condemnation) by [Himself] becoming a curse for us, for it is written [in the Scriptures], Cursed is everyone who hangs on a tree (is crucified).

John 3:16, 17, NKJV

For God so loved the world that He gave His only begotten Son, that whoever believes in Him should not perish but have everlasting life. For God did not send His Son into the world to condemn the world, but that the world through Him might be saved.

Roman 5:8, NKJV

But God demonstrates His own love toward us, in that while we were still sinners, Christ died for us.

Ephesians 2:4, 5, NIV

But because of His great love for us, God, who is rich in mercy, made us alive with Christ even when we were dead in transgressions—it is by grace you have been saved.

Ephesians 2:8–10, NKJV

For by grace you have been saved through faith, and that not of yourselves; it is the gift of God, not of works, lest anyone should boast. For we are His workmanship, created in Christ Jesus for good works, which God prepared beforehand that we should walk in them.

8. Guard the Heart—"I Am Who God Says I Am"

I guard my heart, for as I think in my heart, so shall I become.
I am who God says I am. I am destined to become like Jesus.
I choose to believe the faithfulness of His Word, and by doing so **I choose LIFE**, for His Word preserves my life.

Proverbs 4:20–23, NIV

Pay attention to what I say; listen closely to my words. Do not let them out of your sight, keep them within your heart; **for they are life to those who find them** and health to a man's whole body. Above all else, **guard your heart**, for it is the wellspring of life.

Proverbs 23:7, AMP

For as he thinks in his heart, so is he.

Romans 8:28, 29, NKJV

And we know that all things work together for good to those who love God, to those who are the called according to His purpose. For whom He foreknew, He also predestined to be conformed to the image of His Son.

Deuteronomy 30:19, NKJV

I call heaven and earth as witnesses today against you, that I have set before you life and death, blessing and cursing; therefore choose life.

Deuteronomy 32:46, 47, NIV

Take to heart all the words I have solemnly declared to you. . . . They are not just idle words for you—they are your life.

Psalm 119:37, NIV

Preserve my life according to your word.

Isaiah 26:3, NKJV

You will keep him in perfect peace, whose mind is stayed on You, because he trusts in You.

Luke 6:45, NIV

The good man brings good things out of the good stored up in his heart, and the evil man brings evil things out of the evil stored up in his heart. For out of the overflow of his heart his mouth speaks.

9. Partaking of the Divine Nature

I am partaking of God's divine nature by holding fast to His promises.
I am planting God's promises in my heart to ensure I don't sin against Him.
All of God's promises are mine, "yes" and "amen" ("so be it"), *in Christ.*
I eagerly anticipate the fulfillment of God's promises. This hope is an anchor for my soul, keeping me from being double-minded. Through obedience, faith, and patience, I am confident I will receive what my Father has promised.

2 Peter 1:3, 4, NIV

His divine power has given us everything we need for life and godliness through our knowledge of him who called us by his own glory and goodness. . . . He has given us **his very great and precious promises,** so that **through them you may participate in the divine nature** and escape the corruption in the world caused by evil desires.

Psalm 119:11, NKJV

Your word I have hidden in my heart, that I might not sin against You!

2 Corinthians 1:20, NIV

For no matter how many promises God has made, they are "Yes" in Christ.

Hebrews 6:17–19, NIV

Because God wanted to make the unchanging nature of his purpose very clear to the heirs of what was promised, he confirmed it with an oath. God did this so that, by two unchangeable things in which it is impossible for God to lie, we who have fled to take hold of the hope offered to us may be greatly encouraged. **We have this hope as an anchor for the soul, firm and secure.**

Hebrews 10:36–38, NKJV

For you have need of endurance, so that **after you have done the will of God, you may receive the promise:** "For yet a little while, And He who is coming will come and will not tarry." Now the just shall live by faith; but if anyone draws back, My soul has no pleasure in him.

Hebrews 6:12, NKJV

Do not become sluggish, but imitate those who **through faith and patience inherit the promises.**

10. Believe and Speak—the "Spirit of Faith"

I have been given the **spirit of faith**, which boldly proclaims, *"I believe, therefore I have spoken."*

I confess my hope, speaking *from* faith and *in* faith.

2 Corinthians 4:13, NKJV

And since we have the same **spirit of faith,** according to what is written, "I believed and therefore I spoke," we also believe and therefore speak.

Hebrews 10:23, AMP

So let us seize and hold fast and retain without wavering the hope we cherish and confess and our acknowledgement of it, for He who promised is reliable (sure) and faithful to His word.

11. Anointed Desire, Decisions, and Determination

I am anointed by the Holy One. God works in me to cause me to—

- **desire** the right choices,
- **decide** to follow His instructions, and
- **determine** to act as He planned for His good purpose.

I walk in **deliberate devotion** to Him. I simply "yield," and He does the rest!

2 Corinthians 1:21, 22, NIV
Now it is God who makes both us and you stand firm in Christ. **He anointed us**, set his seal of ownership on us, and put his Spirit in our hearts as a deposit, guaranteeing what is to come.

1 John 2:20, 27, NIV
But **you have an anointing** from the Holy One, and all of you know the truth. As for you, the anointing you received from him remains in you, and you do not need anyone to teach you. But as his anointing teaches you about all things and as that anointing is real, not counterfeit—just as it has taught you, remain in him.

Philippians 2:13, NIV
For **it is God who works in you** to will and to act according to his good purpose.

12. Guard the Mouth—Tongue Power

I guard my mouth. The power of life and death is in my tongue.
I believe in my heart, but it is my spoken *confession* of His Word that releases His power into my life. I speak in faith—and not in doubt and disbelief.
I speak God's Word over my life and know that He is watching to perform it.

Psalm 141:3, NKJV

Set a guard, O Lord, over my mouth; keep watch over the door of my lips.

Proverbs 18:21, NIV

The tongue has the power of life and death, and those who love it will eat its fruit.

Numbers 14:28, NKJV

Say to them, "As I live," says the Lord, "just as you have spoken in My hearing, so I will do to you."

Proverbs 21:23, NKJV

Whoever guards his mouth and tongue keeps his soul from troubles.

Romans 10:8–10, NIV

The word is near you; it is in your mouth and in your heart, that is, the **word of faith** we are proclaiming: That if you confess with your mouth, "Jesus is Lord," and believe in your heart that God raised him from the dead, you will be saved. For it is with your heart that you believe and are justified, and it is with your **mouth** that you **confess and are saved**.

Hebrews 10:23, NKJV

Let us hold fast the confession of our hope without wavering, for He who promised is faithful.

2 Corinthians 4:13, NIV

It is written: "I believed; therefore I have spoken." With that same spirit of faith we also believe and therefore speak.

Isaiah 50:4, AMP

The Lord God has given me the tongue of disciples and of those who are taught, that I should know how to speak a word in season to him who is weary.

Jeremiah 1:12, AMP

Then said the Lord to me, You have seen well, for I am alert and active, watching over My word to perform it.

13. Two-Edged Sword Authority

He has given me the authority and eternal power of His Word.

His Word is alive, active, immovable, and unshakable.

His Word is a two-edged sword—
the first edge struck when He spoke it;
the second edge strikes when I speak it.

As I speak the Word, I hear the voice of the Lord.

I am returning His Word to Him and His Word does not return void, but accomplishes every purpose for which He sent it.

He actively watches over His Word to make certain it is fulfilled at the perfect time which He has appointed.

Hebrews 4:12, NKJV

For the word of God is **living and powerful**, and sharper than any two-edged sword, piercing even to the division of soul and spirit, and of joints and marrow, and is a discerner of the thoughts and intents of the heart.

Isaiah 55:9–11, 13, NIV

As the heavens are higher than the earth, so are my ways higher than your ways and my thoughts than your thoughts. As the rain and the snow come down from heaven, and do not return to it without watering the earth and making it bud and flourish, so that it yields seed for the sower and bread for the eater, **so is my Word that goes out from my mouth: It will not return to me empty, but will accomplish what I desire and achieve the purpose for which I sent it.** . . . This will be for the LORD's renown, for an everlasting sign, which will not be destroyed.

Jeremiah 1:12, AMP

Then said the Lord to me, You have seen well, for I am alert and active, **watching over My word to perform it.**

Luke 1:20, AMP

But My words are of a kind which will be fulfilled in the appointed and proper time.

Habakkuk 2:3, AMP

For the vision is yet for **an appointed time** and it hastens to the end [fulfillment]; it will not deceive or disappoint. Though it tarry, wait [earnestly] for it, because it will surely come, it will not be behindhand on its appointed day.

14. Walking in Christ's Footsteps

His Word is a lamp unto my feet and helps me to walk in Christ's footsteps.
His Word illuminates my path and shows me the direction of my future steps.
He sustains me with His powerful Word.

Psalm 119:105, NKJV

Your word is a lamp to my feet and a light to my path.

Proverbs 4:18, NKJV

But the path of the just is like the shining sun, that shines ever brighter unto the perfect day.

Colossians 2:6, AMP

As you have therefore received the Christ . . . walk—regulate your lives and conduct yourselves—in union with and conformity to Him.

1 John 2:6, NIV

Whoever claims to live in him must walk as Jesus did.

2 John 6, NIV

And this is love: that we walk in obedience to his commands. . . . his command is that you walk in love.

John 8:12, NIV

When Jesus spoke again to the people, he said, "I am the light of the world. Whoever follows me will never walk in darkness, but will have the light of life."

Psalm 89:15, NIV

Blessed are those who have learned to acclaim you, who walk in the light of your presence, O Lord.

Psalm 85:13, NKJV

Righteousness will go before Him, and shall make His footsteps our pathway.

Hebrews 1:3, AMP

He [Jesus] is the sole expression of the glory of God—the Light-being, the out-raying of the divine—and He is the perfect imprint *and* very image of [God's] nature, **upholding** *and* **maintaining** *and* **guiding** *and* **propelling the universe by His mighty word of power.**

15. Righteousness of God in Christ

I am the righteousness of God *in Christ Jesus.* God has credited Christ's righteousness to me. Righteousness by faith is the only righteousness that exists. Being made righteous, I now put it into practice by following God's way of thinking and acting. I am obeying His commandments, by His righteousness within me.

2 Corinthians 5:21, NIV

God made him who had no sin to be sin for us, so that in him we might become the **righteousness** of God.

1 Corinthians 1:30, AMP

But it is from Him that you have your life **in Christ Jesus**, Whom God made . . . **our Righteousness** *and thus* making us upright and putting us in right standing with God.

Isaiah 64:6, NKJV

But we are all like an unclean thing, and all our righteousnesses are like filthy rags.

Jeremiah 23:6, NKJV

Now this is His name . . . **THE LORD OUR RIGHTEOUSNESS.**

Isaiah 61:10, NKJV

My soul shall be joyful in my God; For He has clothed me with the garments of salvation, He has covered me with the robe of righteousness.

Roman 5:17, NKJV

Those who receive abundance of grace and of the gift of righteousness will reign in life through the One, Jesus Christ.

Romans 9:30, NKJV

Gentiles, who did not pursue righteousness, have attained to righteousness, even the righteousness of faith.

1 John 2:29, NKJV

If you know that He is righteous, you know that everyone who practices righteousness is born of Him.

Psalm 85:13, NKJV

Righteousness will go before Him, and shall make His footsteps our pathway.

1 John 3:7, 8, NKJV

Little children, let no one deceive you. **He who practices righteousness is righteous, just as He is righteous.** He who sins is of the devil. . . . For this purpose the Son of God was manifested, that He might destroy the works of the devil.

16. Blessed and Equipped to Do His Will

In Christ Jesus, I have already been blessed with every spiritual blessing and equipped with everything good for doing His will and pleasing Him in every way. God is working to teach me His will and to cause me to desire that His will be done.

I must turn my willingness into resolve. The Lord does not force me to act. I must take that first "step of faith," and then the power of God shows up to cause me to act according to His good purposes.

I fully recognize my life is dedicated to the Lord—yet I still may fail to dedicate each day to Him. Day by day, I must choose to walk with Him.

Ephesians 1:3, NIV

Praise be to the God and Father of our LORD Jesus Christ, who has blessed us in the heavenly realms with every spiritual blessing in Christ.

2 Peter 1:3, 4, NIV

His divine power has given us everything we need for life and godliness through our knowledge of him who called us by his own glory and goodness. Through these he has given us his very great and precious promises, so that through them you may participate in the divine nature and escape the corruption in the world caused by evil desires.

Hebrews 13:20, 21, NKJV

Now may the God of peace who brought up our LORD Jesus from the dead, that great Shepherd of the sheep, through the blood of the everlasting covenant, make you complete in every good work to do His will, working in you what is well pleasing in His sight, through Jesus Christ, to whom be glory forever and ever. Amen.

1 Thessalonians 5:23, 24, NKJV

Now may the God of peace Himself sanctify you completely; and may your whole spirit, soul, and body be preserved blameless at the coming of our LORD Jesus Christ. He who calls you is faithful, who also will do it.

Philippians 2:13, NKJV

For it is God who works in you both to will and to do for His good pleasure.

Joshua 24:15, NKJV

Choose for yourselves this day whom you will serve.

17. Plugging In to Your Power Source

By the power of His Word and His Holy Spirit, my Father lights up every area of my life and eliminates the darkness of my soul.

He lights the lamp of my inner being and causes me to shine with His radiance.

I stay "plugged in" to my power source, and He gives my life true purpose.

Psalm 119:130, NKJV

The entrance of Your words gives light; it gives understanding to the simple.

Psalm 18:28, NKJV

For You will light my lamp; the LORD my God will enlighten my darkness.

Ephesians 5:14, AMP

Therefore He says, Awake, O sleeper, and arise from the dead, and Christ shall shine [make day dawn] upon you and give you light.

Isaiah 60:1, AMP

Arise [from the depression and prostration in which circumstances have kept you; rise to a new life]! **Shine**—be radiant with the glory of the Lord; **for your light has come,** and the glory of the Lord has risen upon you!

18. Beholding—Becoming

I am beholding the Lamb of God, focusing on His love, life, light, and power! I become what I behold. (I develop character traits of the one who occupies my attention.) **I will focus on His strengths** rather than on my weaknesses!

John 1:29, NKJV

"Behold! The Lamb of God who takes away the sin of the world!"

Hebrews 12:2, NIV

Let us fix our eyes on Jesus, the author and perfecter of our faith.

Psalm 17:15

As for me, I will behold thy face in righteousness: I shall be satisfied, when I awake, with thy likeness.

2 Corinthians 12:9, 10, NIV

But He said to me, "My grace is sufficient for you, **for my power is made perfect in weakness.**" Therefore I will boast all the more gladly about my weaknesses, so that Christ's power may rest on me. . . . For when I am weak, then I am strong.

19. Spiritual Armor

He has given me powerful spiritual armor.

Daily, I put on the belt of truth—*which is the reliability of God's Word.*

I put on the breastplate of righteousness—*the righteousness of Christ that God has credited to my account on the basis of my being positioned in Christ Jesus and through my faith in Him.*

My feet are fitted with the readiness of the gospel—*my footing is secure on the foundation of Christ and I have inner peace based on God's message of redemption.*

I use the shield of faith—*faith in God's character, His Word, and His ability to perform His Word.*

I put on the helmet of salvation—*blessed assurance that protects my mind, knowing salvation flows from His grace and is my gift from God.*

I am using the powerful sword of the Spirit—*the rhema word of God that I confess and practice in my life.*

And, I gain an audience with God through the power of prayer—*giving God permission to intervene and release His power into all situations.*

I stand firm in faith.

Ephesians 6:13–18, NKJV

Therefore take up the whole armor of God, that you may be able to withstand in the evil day, and having done all, to stand. Stand therefore, having girded your waist with truth, having put on the breastplate of righteousness, and having shod your feet with the preparation of the gospel of peace; above all, taking the shield of faith with which you will be able to quench all the fiery darts of the wicked one. And take the helmet of salvation, and the sword of the Spirit, which is the word of God; praying always with all prayer and supplication in the Spirit, being watchful to this end with all perseverance and supplication for all the saints.

Isaiah 7:9, NIV

If you do not stand firm in your faith, you will not stand at all.

20. Assurance of Hope—It Is Written

I am sure of what I hope for, and certain the things I do not yet see will happen. "It is written," and God watches to assure His Word is fulfilled.

Trust is the foundation for my hope and faith. I trust God completely and put my hope in His Word, eagerly anticipating the fulfillment of His promises in my life.

Nothing can sway me from the truth—my soul is well anchored. I live by faith, which is my "title deed" to God's promises. My faith is made operative by my actions of obedience.

Obedience is the pathway to God's blessings.

Hebrews 6:18, 19, NIV

We who have fled to take hold of the hope offered to us may be greatly encouraged. We have this hope as an anchor for the soul, firm and secure.

Habakkuk 2:2, 3, AMP

And the Lord answered me and said, Write the vision and engrave it so plainly upon tablets that everyone who passes may be able to read [it easily and quickly] as he hastens by. For the vision is yet for an appointed time and it hastens to the end [fulfillment]; it will not deceive or disappoint. Though it tarry, wait [earnestly] for it, because it will surely come; it will not be behindhand on its appointed day.

Jeremiah 1:12, AMP

Then the Lord said to me, You have seen well, for I am alert and active, watching over My word to perform it.

Hebrews 11:1, AMP

Now faith is the assurance (the confirmation, the title-deed) of the things [we] hope for, being the proof of things [we] do not see and the conviction of their reality—faith perceiving as real fact what is not revealed to the senses.

James 2:17, AMP

So also faith if it does not have works (deeds and actions of obedience to back it up), by itself is destitute of power—inoperative, dead.

Hebrews 10:36, NIV

When you have done the will of God, you will receive what he has promised.

21. Take Up Your Cross

I take up my cross daily in deliberate determination to crucify my old "sin nature." By the power of the Holy Spirit, I put to death my old way of life and bury it. I clothe myself with Christ that I might live a resurrected lifestyle. My earnest prayer is that I will be **continually filled** with the Holy Spirit. I am learning to live in the power of Christ's resurrection, by the divine nature of Christ living in me.

Luke 9:23, NKJV

Then He said to them all, "If anyone desires to come after Me, let him deny himself, and take up his cross daily, and follow Me."

Romans 8:13, NKJV

By the Spirit you put to death the deeds of the body.

Romans 6:4–6, NKJV

Therefore we were buried with Him through baptism into death, that just as Christ was raised from the dead by the glory of the Father, **even so we also should walk in newness of life.** For if we have been united together in the likeness of His death, certainly we also shall be in the likeness of His resurrection, knowing this, that our old man was crucified with Him, that the body of sin might be done away with, that we should no longer be slaves of sin.

Romans 13:14, NKJV

But put on the Lord Jesus Christ, and make no provision for the flesh, to fulfill its lusts.

Ephesians 5:18, AMP

Ever be filled and stimulated with the (Holy) Spirit.

Romans 6:11, AMP

Even so consider yourselves also **dead to sin** and your relation to it broken, **but [that you are] alive to God**—living in unbroken fellowship with Him—in Christ Jesus.

Philippians 3:10, 11, NIV

I want to **know Christ** and the **power of his resurrection** and the fellowship of sharing in his sufferings, becoming like him in his death, and so, somehow, to attain to the resurrection from the dead.

Colossians 1:27, NKJV

To them God willed to make known . . . the riches of the glory of this mystery . . . which is Christ in you, the hope of glory.

22. An Unquenchable Desire for His Word

I have an unquenchable desire for the inexhaustible Word of God.
As a disciple of Jesus Christ, the Messiah, I live in (and according to) His Word. Because I adhere to His teachings, I have an intimate knowledge through personal experience of the truth—and His truth has set me free!

Psalm 42:1, 2, NIV

As the deer pants for streams of water, so my soul pants for you, O God. My soul thirsts for God, for the living God. When can I go and meet with God?

Jeremiah 15:16, NKJV

Your words were found, and I ate them, and Your word was to me the joy and rejoicing of my heart; for I am called by Your name, O LORD God of hosts.

Psalm 119:103, NKJV

How sweet are Your words to my taste, sweeter than honey to my mouth!

Job 23:12, NKJV

I have not departed from the commandment of His lips; I have treasured the words of His mouth more than my necessary food.

Matthew 4:4, NKJV

"It is written, 'Man shall not live by bread alone, but by every word that proceeds from the mouth of God.' "

Psalm 119:11, NKJV

Your word I have hidden in my heart, that I might not sin against You!

John 8:31, 32, AMP

So Jesus said . . . , **If** you **abide** in My Word—hold fast to My teachings and live in accordance with them—**you are truly My disciples.** And you will know the truth, and the truth will set you free.

John 8:36, NIV

So if the Son sets you free, you will be free indeed.

Psalm 119:32, NIV

I run in the path of your commands, for you have set my heart free.

Romans 6:22, 23, AMP

But now since you have been set free from sin and have become the slaves of God, you have your present reward in holiness and its end is eternal life. For the wages which sin pays is death, but the [bountiful] free gift of God is eternal life through (in union with) Jesus Christ our Lord.

23. Renewed Mind—Changed Attitudes—the Mind of Christ

My mind is renewed—my attitudes are made new (and radically changed) through the power of His Word. His Word sanctifies me, separating me from the world's viewpoint. I am set apart morally, ethically, and attitudinally from the world system. My conduct and my thoughts are governed by God's administrative system of His holy kingdom, as recorded in His Word.

I am re-created in the image of God. I have been given the mind of Christ.

By the power of the Holy Spirit, I take every thought captive and make it obedient to the will of Christ, my Lord.

Romans 12:2, NKJV

And do not be conformed to this world, but be transformed by the renewing of your mind, that you may prove what is that good and acceptable and perfect will of God.

John 17:17, NKJV

Sanctify them by Your truth. Your word is truth.

Ephesians 4:22–24, AMP

Strip yourselves of your former nature—put off and discard your old unrenewed self—which characterized your previous manner of life and becomes corrupt through lusts and desires that spring from delusion. And be constantly renewed in the spirit of your mind—having a fresh mental and spiritual attitude—**and put on the new nature (the regenerate self) created in God's image,** (Godlike) in true righteousness and holiness.

Ephesians 2:10, AMP

For we are God's [own] handiwork (His workmanship), recreated in Christ Jesus, [born anew] that we may do those good works which God predestined (planned beforehand) for us.

1 Corinthians 2:16, NKJV

We have the mind of Christ.

2 Corinthians 10:4, 5, NKJV

For the weapons of our warfare are not carnal but mighty in God for pulling down strongholds, casting down arguments and every high thing that exalts itself against the knowledge of God, bringing every thought into captivity to the obedience of Christ.

24. Chosen, Redeemed, and Worth Nothing Less Than the Price He Paid

I am a chosen and redeemed person. Jesus paid a price of unspeakable value for me. **I am worth nothing less than the price He paid.** I am bought, paid for, and covered by the precious blood of Jesus. He has made me a member of a royal priesthood, a special person belonging to the Lord. I walk in the marvelous light of His kingdom, and God grants me favor with every-one.

1 Peter 1:18, 19, AMP

You must know (recognize) that you were redeemed (ransomed) from the useless (fruitless) way of living inherited by tradition from [your] forefathers, . . . not with corruptible things [such as] silver and gold, **But [you were purchased] with the precious blood of Christ,** the Messiah, like that of a [sacrificial] lamb without blemish or spot.

1 Corinthians 6:19, 20, NIV

Do you not know that your body is a temple of the Holy Spirit, who is in you, whom you have received from God? You are not your own; **you were bought at a price.** Therefore honor God with your body.

1 Peter 2:9, 10, NKJV

But you are a chosen generation, a royal priesthood, a holy nation, His own special people, that you may proclaim the praises of Him who called you out of darkness into His marvelous light; who once were not a people but are now the people of God, who had not obtained mercy but now have obtained mercy.

1 John 1:7, NKJV

But if we walk in the light as He is in the light, we have fellowship with one another, and the blood of Jesus Christ His Son cleanses us from all sin.

Psalm 5:12, NKJV

For You, O LORD, will bless the righteous; with favor You will surround him as with a shield.

Psalm 84:11, NKJV

For the LORD God is a sun and shield; the LORD will give grace and glory; no good thing will He withhold from those who walk uprightly.

Proverbs 3:3, 4, NIV

Let love and faithfulness never leave you; bind them around your neck, write them on the tablet of your heart. Then you will win favor and a good name in the sight of God and man.

25. Love the Lord With All Your Heart, Soul, Mind, and Strength

I love the Lord my God with all my **heart**, **soul**, **mind**, and **strength**. Even in this response to Him, I am totally dependent upon God. God is the source of love.

I open my heart and allow Him to pour His love into me. God empowers me to respond in love. I am always mindful of Jesus Christ, my "First Love."

Mark 12:28–30, NIV

One of the teachers of the law came and . . . asked him, "Of all the commandments, which is the most important?" "The most important one," answered Jesus, "is this: 'Hear, O Israel, the Lord our God, the Lord is one. Love the Lord your God with all your **heart** and with all your **soul** and with all your **mind** and with all your **strength**.' "

Romans 5:5, NKJV

The love of God has been poured out in our hearts by the Holy Spirit who was given to us.

Revelation 2:3–5, NIV

You have persevered and have endured hardships for my name, and have not grown weary. Yet I hold this against you: **You have forsaken your first love.** Remember the height from which you have fallen! Repent and do the things you did at first.

26. Zealous and Burning Desire

I am always zealous for the things of God. The Holy Spirit gives me a burning desire to serve the Lord in earnest and with perseverance.

Romans 12:11, AMP

Never lag in zeal and in earnest endeavor; be aglow and burning with the Spirit, serving the Lord.

Galatians 6:9, AMP

And let us not lose heart and grow weary and faint in acting nobly and doing right, for in due time and at the appointed season we shall reap, if we do not loosen and relax our courage and faint.

Hebrews 10:36, NKJV

For you have need of endurance, so that after you have done the will of God, you may receive the promise.

27. Demonstrate Your Love for God Through Obedience

This is how I demonstrate my love for God—
I obey His commandments.
I put **His Word into practice.**
I am held accountable for that which He has revealed to me.

John 14:15, NKJV
If you love Me, keep My commandments.

1 John 5:3, 4, NIV
This is love for God: **to obey his commands.** And his commands are not burdensome, for everyone born of God overcomes the world. This is the victory that has overcome the world, even our faith.

Luke 8:21, NIV
He replied, "My mother and brothers are those who **hear** God's word and **put it into practice.**"

Luke 11:28, AMP
But He said, **Blessed** . . . rather are they who hear the Word of God and **obey** and **practice** it!

Philippians 3:16, AMP
Only let us hold true to what we have already attained *and* walk *and* order our lives by that.

1 Corinthians 4:2, NIV
Now it is required that those who have been given a trust must prove faithful.

Romans 14:23, AMP
For whatever does not originate *and* proceed from faith is sin—that is, whatever is done without a conviction of its **approval by God** is sinful.

1 John 2:3, 4, NKJV
Now by this we know that we know Him, if we keep His commandments. He who says, "I know Him," and does not keep His commandments, is a liar, and the truth is not in him.

Deuteronomy 28:13, NKJV
And the LORD will make you the head and not the tail; you shall be above only, and not be beneath, if you heed the commandments of the LORD your God, which I command you today, and are careful to observe them."

28. Search Me and Show Me Where I Fall Short

Holy and righteous Father, please search my heart and mind.
Show me the areas in which I fall short of Your glory.
Please lead me to godly sorrow and repentance. Please wash me thoroughly and repeatedly in the precious blood of Jesus and cleanse me of my sin.
I want to know Jesus Christ and the power of His resurrection.
I want to be more like Jesus.
Create in me a pure heart and consistent actions of faith.
I rely on Your power to be made perfect in my weakness.

Psalm 139:23, 24, NIV

Search me, O God, and know my heart; test me and know my anxious thoughts. See if there is any offensive way in me, and lead me in the way everlasting.

Psalm 19:12, AMP

Clear me from hidden [and unconscious] faults.

Romans 3:23, NKJV

For all have sinned and fall short of the glory of God, being justified freely by His grace through the redemption that is in Christ Jesus.

2 Corinthians 7:10, NIV

Godly sorrow brings repentance that leads to salvation and leaves no regret.

Psalm 51:2, AMP

Wash me thoroughly [and repeatedly] from my iniquity and guilt and cleanse me and make me wholly pure from my sin.

1 John 1:7, NKJV

But if we walk in the light as He is in the light, we have fellowship with one another, and the blood of Jesus Christ His Son cleanses us from all sin.

Philippians 3:10, NIV

I want to know Christ and the power of his resurrection.

2 Corinthians 12:9, NIV

He said to me, "My grace is sufficient for you, for my power is made perfect in weakness."

29. Confessed Sins—Washed of Uncleanness

With a humble heart, I daily confess my sins. In sincere repentance and turning away from sin, I am forgiven. The blood of Christ cleanses me of all unrighteousness. He cancels and blots out my transgressions for His own sake.

His grace is sufficient to cover all my sins, and He remembers them no more.

Ezekiel 18:21, 22, NKJV

But if a wicked man turns from all his sins . . . keeps all My statutes, and does what is lawful and right, he shall surely live; he shall not die. **None** of the transgressions which he has committed shall be remembered against him.

1 John 1:7–9, NKJV

But if we walk in the light as He is in the light . . . the blood of Jesus Christ His Son cleanses us from all sin. If we say that we have no sin, we deceive ourselves, and the truth is not in us. **If we confess our sins, He is faithful and just to forgive us our sins and to cleanse us from all unrighteousness.**

Hebrews 8:10–12, NIV

This is the covenant . . . I will put my laws in their minds and write them on their hearts. I will be their God, and they will be my people . . . they will all know me . . . **I will forgive their wickedness and will remember their sins no more.**

Ephesians 1:7, NKJV

In Him we have redemption through His blood, the forgiveness of sins, according to the riches of His grace.

2 Corinthians 12:9, NIV

My grace is sufficient for you.

Isaiah 43:25, AMP

I, even I, am He Who blots out and cancels your transgressions, for My own sake, and **I will not remember** your sins.

Psalm 103:12, NKJV

As far as the east is from the west, so far has He removed our transgressions from us.

Isaiah 44:22, NKJV

I have blotted out, like a thick cloud, your transgressions, and like a cloud, your sins. Return to Me, for I have redeemed you.

1 Kings 14:8, NKJV

You have not been as My servant David, who kept My commandments and who followed Me with all his heart, to do only what was right in My eyes. (Author's note: God spoke this after David's death, demonstrating that the Lord forgot the sins David asked Him to forgive.)

30. Perfect Peace

I am walking in constant peace—His peace that guards my heart in all circumstances and that is beyond human understanding. **God keeps me in perfect peace,** because my mind has a steadfast trust in His faithfulness.

Whenever I begin to feel stressed and anxious, I realize my eyes are not focused on my Lord. I return my thoughts to Him and place my complete trust in Him.

He restores my peace, causing me to overflow with hope by the power of His Spirit.

Philippians 4:6, NKJV

Be anxious for nothing, but in everything by prayer and supplication, with thanksgiving, let your requests be made known to God; and **the peace of God**, which surpasses all understanding, will guard your hearts and minds through Christ Jesus.

Isaiah 26:3, NKJV

You will keep him in **perfect peace**, whose mind is stayed on You, because he trusts in You.

1 Corinthians 14:33

For God is not the author of confusion, but of peace.

John 14:27, AMP

Peace I leave with you; My [own] peace I now give and bequeath to you. Not as the world gives do I give to you. Do not let your heart be troubled, neither let it be afraid.

Isaiah 30:15, AMP

For thus said the Lord God, the Holy One of Israel: In returning *to Me* and resting *in Me* you shall be saved; in quietness and in [trusting] confidence shall be your strength.

Isaiah 32:17, NIV

The fruit of righteousness will be **peace**; the effect of righteousness will be quietness and confidence forever.

Romans 15:13, NIV

May the God of hope fill you with all **joy and peace** as you trust in him, so that you may overflow with hope by the power of the Holy Spirit.

31. All Things Are Possible Through the Strength of Christ

All things are possible with God. **I can do all things through Christ Jesus,** who keeps on strengthening me with His sufficiency and with His power, through His Spirit in my innermost being.

The power of His Holy Presence is working in me, and He will perfect His strength in me to overcome my weaknesses.

My flesh counts for nothing! Only His Spirit brings real life!

Matthew 19:26, NKJV

But Jesus looked at them and said to them, "With men this is impossible, but with God all things are possible."

Philippians 4:13, NKJV

I can do all things through Christ who strengthens me.

Philippians 4:13, AMP

I have strength for all things in Christ who empowers me—I am ready for anything and equal to anything through Him who infuses inner strength into me.

Ephesians 3:16, NIV

I pray that out of his glorious riches **he may strengthen you with power** through his Spirit in your inner being.

Ephesians 3:16, AMP

May He grant you out of the rich treasury of His glory to be **strengthened** and reinforced **with mighty power** in the inner man by the (Holy) Spirit [Himself]— indwelling your innermost being and personality.

Colossians 1:11, AMP

[We pray] that you may be invigorated and strengthened with **all power** according to the might of His glory, [to exercise] every kind of endurance and patience . . . with joy.

2 Corinthians 12:9, NIV

But He said to me, "My grace is sufficient for you, for my power is made perfect in weakness."

Galatians 3:3, NKJV

Are you so foolish? Having begun in the Spirit, are you now being made perfect by the flesh?

John 6:63, AMP

It is the Spirit who gives life—He is the Life-giver; the flesh conveys no benefit whatever—there is no profit in it. The words (truths) that I have been speaking to you are spirit and life.

32. Plans Committed to Him Succeed

Whatever I do, I commit my plans to the Lord and He causes them to succeed. My hard work brings a profit. My success increases because I have many godly advisors. I commit my days into God's hands—He directs me and gives me strength and power for a victorious life.

Proverbs 16:3, NIV

Commit to the LORD whatever you do, and your plans will succeed.

Psalm 127:1, NKJV

Unless the LORD builds the house, they labor in vain who build it; unless the LORD guards the city, the watchman stays awake in vain.

Psalm 37:5–7, NKJV

Commit your way to the LORD, trust also in Him, and He shall bring it to pass. He shall bring forth your righteousness as the light, and your justice as the noonday. Rest in the LORD, and wait patiently for Him.

Proverbs 14:23, NIV

All hard work brings a profit, but mere talk leads only to poverty.

Proverbs 15:22, NIV

Plans fail for lack of counsel, but with many advisers they succeed.

Isaiah 48:17, 18, NKJV

"I am the LORD your God, who teaches you to profit, who leads you by the way you should go. Oh, that you had heeded My commandments! Then your peace would have been like a river, and your righteousness like the waves of the sea."

Deuteronomy 8:17, 18, NKJV

Then you say in your heart, "My power and the might of my hand have gained me this wealth." And you shall remember the LORD your God, for it is He who gives you power to get wealth, that He may establish His covenant which He swore to your fathers, as it is this day.

1 Chronicles 29:11–13, AMP

Yours, O Lord, is the greatness, and the power, and the glory, and the victory, and the majesty; for all that is in the heavens and the earth is Yours; Yours is the kingdom, O Lord, and Yours it is to be exalted as head over all. **Both riches and honor come from**

You, and You reign over all. **In Your hands are power and might; in Your hand it is to make great and to give strength to all. Now therefore, our God, we thank You and praise Your glorious name** and those attributes which that name denotes.

33. God-Given Health

It is the name (representing all He is) of Jesus Christ and the faith that comes **through Him** that gives me complete healing. I follow God's instructions for health and healing. The Lord, Jehovah-rapha, is my Counselor and Healer. By His grace, I am walking in God-given health (spiritually, mentally, emotionally, and physically). I trust God to give me the healing that He knows I need. He has my eternal benefit in mind. He took up my infirmities and carried all my diseases. He sent His living Word, Jesus Christ, who was bruised for my iniquities. By His stripes I was healed!

Acts 3:16, NIV

By faith in the name of Jesus, this man whom you see and know was made strong. **It is Jesus' name and the faith that comes through him** that has given this **complete healing** to him, as you can all see.

Exodus 15:26, NKJV

If you diligently heed the voice of the Lord your God and do what is right in His sight, give ear to His commandments and keep all His statutes, I will put none of the diseases on you. . . . For I am the Lord who heals you.

Psalm 103:2, 3, NKJV

Bless the Lord, O my soul, and forget not all His benefits: who forgives all your iniquities, who heals all your diseases.

Matthew 8:16, 17, AMP

When evening came, they brought to Him many who were under the power of demons, and He drove out the spirits with a word and restored to health all who were sick. And thus He fulfilled what was spoken by the prophet Isaiah, **He Himself took (in order to carry away) our weaknesses *and* infirmities and bore away our diseases.**

Psalm 107:20, AMP

He sends forth His word and heals them and rescues them from the pit *and* destruction.

Isaiah 53:4, 5, NIV

Surely he took up our infirmities and carried our sorrows, yet we considered him stricken by God, smitten by him, and afflicted. **But he was pierced for our transgressions, he was crushed for our iniquities;** the punishment that brought us peace was upon him, and **by his wounds we are healed.**

1 Peter 2:24, NKJV
Who Himself bore our sins in His own body on the tree, that we, having died to sins, might live for righteousness—by whose stripes you were healed.

34. Comfort Overflowing

God comforts me in all my troubles. He heals my broken heart. **Through Christ, my comfort overflows.** I encourage others with my testimony and share with them the same comfort I have received from the Lord.

2 Corinthians 1:3, 4 NIV

Praise be to the God and Father of our Lord Jesus Christ, the Father of compassion and the God of all comfort, **who comforts us in all our troubles**, so that we can comfort those in any trouble with the comfort we ourselves have received from God.

Psalm 32:7, NKJV

You are my hiding place; You shall preserve me from trouble; You shall surround me with songs of deliverance.

Colossians 3:3, AMP

For [as far as this world is concerned] you have died, and your [new, real] life is hid with Christ in God.

Isaiah 43:1–3, AMP

Fear not, for I have redeemed you—ransomed you by paying a price instead of leaving you captives: I have called you by your name, you are Mine. When you pass through the waters I will be with you, and through the rivers they will not overwhelm you; when you walk through the fire, you shall not be burned or scorched, nor shall the flame kindle upon you. For I am the Lord your God, the Holy One of Israel, your Savior.

Psalm 34:18, NKJV

The LORD is near to those who have a broken heart, and saves such as have a contrite spirit.

Psalm 147:3, AMP

He heals the brokenhearted and binds up their wounds—curing their pains and their sorrows.

Psalm 3:3, AMP

But You, O Lord, are a shield for me, my glory, and the lifter up of my head.

Deuteronomy 33:27, NKJV

The eternal God is your refuge, and underneath are the everlasting arms; He will thrust out the enemy from before you, and will say, "Destroy!"

35. Guard the Ears—the Standard of Truth Is the Bible

I guard my ears. The only message I receive as truth comes from the Word of God.

Faith comes by hearing. Speaking His Word aloud will increase my faith as I listen to my own voice.

Without faith, I cannot please my heavenly Father.

God's promises are ushered into existence by faith.

Mark 4:24, AMP

And He said to them, **Be careful what you are hearing.** The measure [of thought and study] you give [to the truth you hear] will be the measure [of virtue and knowledge] that comes back to you, and more [besides] will be given to you *who* hear.

Isaiah 50:5, 4, AMP

The Lord God has opened My ear, and I have not been rebellious or turned backward. He wakens My ear to hear as disciples—as those who are taught.

Romans 10:17, NIV

Faith comes from hearing the message, and the message is heard through the word of Christ.

Hebrews 11:1, AMP

Now faith is the assurance (the confirmation, the title deed) of the things [we] hope for, being the proof of things [we] do not see and the conviction of their reality—faith perceiving as real fact what is not revealed to the senses.

1 John 5:10, NIV

Anyone who does not believe God has made him out to be a liar.

Hebrews 11:6, NIV

And without faith it is impossible to please God, because anyone who comes to him must believe that he exists and that he rewards those who earnestly seek him.

Hebrews 4:2, AMP

For indeed we have had the glad tidings [of God] proclaimed to us just as truly as they [the Israelites of old did . . .]; **but the message they heard did not benefit them, because it was not mixed with faith . . . by those who heard it.**

36. Spirit of Self-Discipline—Dead to Sin

The Holy Spirit of God lives in me.
I have been given a spirit of power, love, and holiness.
I have been given a spirit of self-discipline and peace.
I have surrendered control of my life to the Spirit of God.
Hallelujah, God has cut me free from the cord of the wicked that tried to bind me.
I am dead to sin, but alive to God.
I am under the power of His grace, and sin shall not be my master.
I have put on Christ Jesus, and I make no provision for my flesh.
God gives me victory through my Lord Jesus Christ.

Romans 8:9, NIV

You, however, are controlled not by the sinful nature but by the Spirit, if the Spirit of God lives in you. And if anyone does not have the Spirit of Christ, he does not belong to Christ.

2 Timothy 1:7, NIV

For God did not give us a spirit of timidity, but a spirit of power, of love and of self-discipline.

1 Corinthians 14:33, NKJV

For God is not the author of confusion but of peace.

Psalm 129:4, NIV

The LORD is righteous; he has cut me free from the cords of the wicked.

1 John 3:8, NKJV

For this purpose the Son of God was manifested, that He might destroy the works of the devil.

Romans 6:11, 14, NKJV

Likewise you also, reckon yourselves to be dead indeed to sin, but alive to God in Christ Jesus our Lord. . . . For sin shall not have dominion over you, for you are not under law but under grace.

Romans 13:14, NKJV

But put on the Lord Jesus Christ, and make no provision for the flesh.

1 Corinthians 15:57, NIV

But thanks be to God! He gives us the victory through our Lord Jesus Christ.

37. Sealed for the Day of Redemption

I am included "in Christ." In Christ, I am sealed for the day of redemption.
Because I remain in Christ (not turning away from Him), absolutely nothing can separate me from the abundant love that God has for me!
I walk hand-in-hand with my Lord. He will not let my foot slip.
No one can snatch me from His hand!
I find complete security in Christ. I will not turn away from Him!
I have died to sin and my true life is hidden with Christ (locked safely in Him).

Ephesians 1:13, 14, NIV

And you also were included in Christ when you heard the word of truth, the gospel of your salvation. Having believed, **you were marked in him with a seal**, **the promised Holy Spirit,** who is a deposit guaranteeing our inheritance until the redemption of those who are God's possession—to the praise of his glory.

Ephesians 4:30, AMP

And do not grieve the Holy Spirit of God (do not offend or vex or sadden Him), by Whom **you were sealed** (marked, branded as God's own, secured) **for the day of redemption**— of final deliverance through Christ from evil and the consequences of sin.

Romans 8:38, 39, NKJV

For I am persuaded that neither death nor life, nor angels nor principalities nor powers, nor things present nor things to come, nor height nor depth, nor any other created thing, shall be able to separate us from the love of God which is in Christ Jesus our Lord.

Psalm 121:3, AMP

He will not allow your foot to slip or to be moved; He Who keeps you will not slumber.

John 10:27–30, NKJV

"My sheep hear My voice, and I know them, and they follow Me. And I give them eternal life, and they shall never perish; neither shall anyone snatch them out of My hand. My Father, who has given them to Me, is greater than all; and no one is able to snatch them out of My Father's hand. I and My Father are one."

Colossians 3:3, NIV

For you died, and **your life is now hidden with Christ** in God.

38. Recognize—Repent—Receive—Rejoice

United with Christ, I am free of guilt and condemnation. I am quick to **RECOGNIZE** when I am not pleasing God and even quicker to **REPENT**. I **RECEIVE** His abundant forgiveness and I **REJOICE** that His compassion is new every morning.

Romans 8:1, 2, NKJV

There is therefore now no condemnation to those who are in Christ Jesus, who do not walk according to the flesh, but according to the Spirit. For the law of the Spirit of life in Christ Jesus has made me free from the law of sin and death.

Revelation 3:1–3, AMP

I know your record and what you are doing; you are supposed to be alive, but [in reality] you are dead. Rouse yourselves and keep awake, and strengthen and invigorate what remains and is on the point of dying; for I have not found a thing that you have done—any work of yours—meeting the requirements of My God or perfect in His sight. **So call to mind the lessons you received and heard; continually lay them to heart and obey them, and repent.** In case you will not rouse yourselves and keep awake and watch, I will come upon you like a thief, and you will not know or suspect at what hour I will come.

Acts 5:30, 31, AMP

The God of our forefathers raised up Jesus . . . God exalted Him to His right hand to be Prince and Leader and Savior and Deliverer and Preserver, in order to **grant repentance** . . . and to **bestow forgiveness** and **release from sins.**

1 John 1:9, NKJV

If we confess our sins, He is faithful and just to forgive us our sins and to cleanse us from all unrighteousness.

Lamentations 3:22, 23, NIV

Because of the LORD's great love we are not consumed, **for his compassions never fail.** They are new every morning; great is your faithfulness.

Start a Word Warrior Squadron

God wants to raise up a multitude of voices exalting His Word. He wants to change our experience in Him. It is our heavenly Father's desire to bestow power from on high, so that He may *cause* us to be what He has *called* us to be.

So that you may become blameless and pure, children of God without fault in a crooked and depraved generation, in which you shine like stars in the universe as you hold out the word of life (Philippians 2:15, 16, NIV).

God is starting a movement of banding small groups of people together to rehearse the practice of speaking life affirmations from Scripture. Each week, these practicing "Word Warriors" meet for an hour to share testimonies and encouragement.

Would you like to share this experience with your church or prayer group? Are you sensing God's call on your life to organize a Word Warrior Squadron?

Word Warrior Ministries has developed a packet of information that will provide guidelines to help you step out in faith in the Word of the Lord. The packet includes tips to promote interest, a meeting agenda, weekly updates of new affirmations, and testimonies of other Word Warrior Squadron groups.

For further information, contact

Word Warrior Ministries
P.O. Box 71
Thompsonville, IL 62890

Email:
info@wordwarriorministries.net

Web site:
www.wordwarriorministries.net